MAN
IN THE
MIDDLE

JOHN AMAECHI
WITH CHRIS BULL

ESPN BOOKS

Author's Note:
Some of the names in this book have been changed to protect privacy.

ISBN-13: 978-1-933060-19-4
ISBN-10: 1-933060-19-0

ESPN books are available for special promotions and premiums.
For details contact Michael Rentas, Assistant Director, Inventory
Operations, Hyperion, 77 West 66th Street, 11th floor, New York,
New York 10023, or call 212-456-0133.

FIRST EDITION

10 9 8 7 6 5 4 3 2 1

MAN

IN THE

MIDDLE

To Mum

A principle is a principle.
And in no case can it be watered down because
of our incapacity to live it in practice.
We have to strive to achieve it, and the striving
should be conscious, deliberate and hard.

—Mahatma Gandhi, 1939

•••] Introduction

And now the man in the middle, from Penn State, John A-meech-eeeeee.

I dash toward center court before it dawns on me that I'm supposed to look cool, as though I'd done this a million times. The game hasn't started, but I am sweating and light-headed. I can barely hear the PA announcer over the roar of the crowd; the burst of flashbulbs adds to my rookie stupefaction.

I glance up at Gund Arena's JumboTron, where my name and image flash in Technicolor. Feeling my way to center court, I join hands with the other starters. As my eyes scan the floor, there's A-M-A-E-C-H-I again, dancing across the floor in laser beams.

Teenaged boasts aside, I'd rarely allowed my mind to imagine actually making it to the NBA. Less than a decade earlier, I was the laughing stock of my public school in Manchester, England—an uncoordinated, hugely overweight nerd with Coke-bottle glasses and no friends. I hadn't even touched a basketball until six years earlier. That part of me still lived inside this newly minted NBA body.

Amid the cacophony, I allow myself a rare flash of satisfaction as my impossible dream becomes reality.

I'm finally here. The N-fuckin'-B-A.

●●●

It was the Cleveland Cavaliers' home opener in November 1995, and I was a 23-year-old rookie center, the first undrafted free agent to make the starting lineup in the history of the league.

We were taking on the Indiana Pacers, but otherwise I was so edgy that the game is nothing more than a blur. I didn't take the tip because, even though I was the tallest member of the team that season, I can't jump over a phone book. (The box score shows I played 12 minutes and scored four points.)

I recall slightly more about my first preseason start, a couple of weeks earlier against mighty Michael Jordan and the Chicago Bulls, mostly because my Penn State pals were watching on a big screen from a rib joint in State College. After the game, they called to congratulate me on my debut, but mostly to tease me about the fact that Scottie Pippen blocked my first NBA shot.

Welcome to the big time, rook!

I laughed out loud at their jibes, secretly afraid to admit that it was actually a proud moment for me just to share a floor with players of Pippen's caliber.

Even my failures now seemed like an honor, and I actually did recover enough from the swat to score a team-leading 12 points (not enough to prevent us from being crushed). I don't even remember being on the floor with Jordan that day in the Peoria Civic Center, but I do recall nailing a sweet hook that seemed to float over Dennis Rodman and two other defenders before settling into the net.

There was reason for my stupefaction. It was hard to comprehend how far I'd come since a British basketball scout stopped me on the street at age 17 and asked whether I'd be interested in basketball. In fact, as I explained, I'd never even touched one. I was officially the worst athlete in a nation not exactly known for its athletic prowess.

And yet, here I was, in this gleaming $130 million arena surrounded by the richest athletes on earth when, six years earlier, my first practice was in a leaky gym with hard-as-concrete floors and baskets affixed to the walls.

While it was hard to come to terms with how far I'd come, I could never have imagined how far I had yet to travel, especially since it is human nature to relax a bit after we have "arrived" at our destination.

I could not have realized that this was the glorious beginning of a pro career that would have as many tragedies as triumphs, as many miscues as miracles, one that would take me on a mind-blowing basketball tour of Europe and America.

Living a more ordinary life in London, I'm only now coming to terms with this journey, three years after I retired as a New York Knick. To be honest, I've always had far more interest in the process of achieving a goal than the goal itself, ever since I'd made a naïve pledge—as a bookworm teenager who'd never even picked up a basketball—to become one of the first Brits to play in the NBA *and* a genuine superstar, following in the footsteps of my heroes Larry Bird, Magic Johnson, and Karl Malone, whose exploits I watched on British television late at night.

I fell far short of that last goal, but I learned plenty of lessons along the way.

From the beginning, the goal had to be achieved in accordance with the document I produced at age 17, with the guidance of my mother—an aspirational experiment we dubbed The Plan.

On one level, The Plan was a handbook for making it to the top of a game I'd only just taken up and at which I was, frankly, terrible. On another level, Mum insisted, Zen-like, that it be a guide not just to fame and fortune but to an ethic of good works. In the unlikely event that I did make it, she insisted it not come at the expense of what she called my "soul in the dark," a contemplative state in which you judge yourself according to what kind of a human being you have become in the process of achieving your goal.

Basically, in no uncertain terms, I was to use whatever basketball status I achieved to become a role model, the term famously rejected but obviously embodied by the great Charles Barkley.

While I certainly fell far short of that lofty (and some might say arrogant) goal, it's one I will spend the rest of my days doing my best to achieve—one that feels far more noble than playing a game that's too often worth nothing more than its entertainment value.

CHAPTER I ●●●] Little Big Man

I haven't always been big.

One of my first memories is the jumbo jet that would take our family to Manchester—and away from the dread that lurked around every corner at 63 Oaks Road in Framingham, Massachusetts.

I was a pint-sized 4-year-old, and the plane was the most massive bird I'd ever seen. Looking through its window, the wings alone seemed to stretch from Boston Harbor all the way across the Atlantic.

That episode remains something of a blur to me. I remember Mum throwing our bags into the back of the car as her best friend—one of our "aunties"—fought back tears while reassuring us that everything would be okay.

I should have been overcome with fear about my disgraced father's threats to hunt us down and make us disappear, the fear of losing a comfortably middle-class existence for a new life in a faraway land. But I was sheltered from the reality of escape in the cover of darkness. Somehow, the trip seemed more of an adventure, the ultimate Hardy Boys caper, than the nightmare it must have been for Mum.

I revelled in this strange and fascinating thing, air travel. The stewardesses doted on me, and presented me with an airline pin and a Coke. I'd fantasized about flying, cheering the antics of the Green Lantern, the superhero whose power ring enabled him to walk through walls and sail through the air.

Now my fantasy was reality.

I knew Mum would never allow me and my younger sisters, Muriel and Uki, to come to harm. Through sheer force of will, she surrounded us with a comforting blanket of security.

In retrospect, I could never have imagined the equally incredible circumstances under which I would return to my country of birth.

As I mull over my family's past, it seems oddly mysterious. Other kids had much more normal, easily understandable origins. Much of my past has been lost to me and, now that Mum's gone, there is no way for me to retrieve it. While she was alive, there was much that remained taboo, things that I felt uncomfortable asking about, even after she became gravely ill.

I'm sorry now about the things I won't know, especially since Mum is the person who was my role model. I measure my strengths as well as my shortcomings by the standards she set.

People who know me now often comment that they wish they had known my mother because I am so obviously a reflection of her. From her I learned perseverance despite great odds, courage in the face of danger, and stoicism against evil.

I measure my strengths as well as my shortcomings by the standards she set.

Mum tried to protect us from the ugliness of those early days by maintaining a steely silence, so there's much her kids don't know. What I do know is based on recollections, letters, and passports I found in an old red suitcase in the back of her bedroom closet after her death, plus the few stories she did share.

My Mum, Wendy Hall, was born in Hyde, a medium-size town in northwest England, in 1945. She grew up wanting be a doctor, but failed her medical school entrance exams the first time around. She was dogged in her pursuit of her goal, a five-foot-nine tower of self-confidence. Redoubling her efforts, she ended up at the remote University of Aberdeen in Scotland, where she got her medical degree and went on to pass the boards her first time around.

She moved to Boston in the 1960s, where she went to work at Mass General Hospital and also worked for a social service group for the poor.

In letters to her parents, she described Boston's tense racial climate of the time. In one, she talked of working with a black nurse who was forced for his own safety to hide under a tarp in the back of Mum's station wagon to avoid being seen in the same car with a white person.

Which makes Mum's own interracial marriage all the more remarkable for its time. From what I've been able to gather, she met my father, Jon Amaechi, in Scotland during medical school, and then traveled with him to his native Nigeria in the 1960s, just as the nation was engulfed in the Biafran war.

Fueled by the political turmoil of the times, they volunteered on behalf of the Ibo, my father's ethnic group, which was facing what today is known as ethnic cleansing. Mum worked as a medic; Dad was a soldier. The assignment was so dangerous that she wrote her parents six months worth of letters before her departure and had them mailed from Boston to Manchester, where her family lived. Later, she was ashamed of this strategy, imagining the trauma she would have inflicted on her parents if they had learned of their only daughter's death and then received a stream of phony letters from beyond the grave.

She never apologized for the mission itself, though. She spoke of her heroic acts as mere necessity: parachuting from planes into battle zones, handgun tucked into her medicine bag; conducting triage as mortar fire erupted around her. She spoke of those days infrequently and with a gravity that made the horror of those experiences uncomfortably real.

When it became clear their faction had lost the conflict and that murderous guerrillas were approaching, my parents fled the country on foot, surviving by eating grubs and other insects they collected along the way. Whenever we would go hiking in the woods years later, she'd make us squirm by pulling grubs out of the bark of a tree and saying, "They only wriggle a little when you eat them!"

After the war, Wendy and Jon settled in Boston, where they married. He started a manufacturing business, while she practiced medicine and raised us.

●••

I was born November 26, 1970; Muriel one year later, Uki a year after that.

It wasn't one big happy family. My father, it turned out, became emotionally abusive to his wife. At one point he signed his business over to Mum without letting her know, ostensibly so she would get the benefit from it. When it teetered on verge of collapse, Dad went back Nigeria, leaving Mum with a mountain of debt. I have no idea how she managed, but she made sure everyone got paid, even though it left us penniless.

Not long after, Dad returned, hoping to win his wife and kids back. Although he stayed in the house for a time, Mum made it clear he was longer part of our family.

A one point Mum landed in the hospital for several weeks with a serious illness. Yet Dad remained distant, refusing to comfort or console us. As his menacing behavior and his veiled contempt escalated, Mum decided it was time to flee to Manchester.

Many years later, I received an e-mail informing me of my father's death. I felt nothing about the loss of the man whose name I bore. I even declined an invitation to speak at his funeral. Children owe a debt to their parents, but being a parent is more than a mere biological contribution. Just as competing in sports is more than just showing up, being a parent means being invested, raising kids with love and respect.

My first major English basketball coach, Joe Forber, is more of a dad to me than my father ever was.

●••

In late 1974 we arrived at my grandparents' home in Stockport, a suburb of Manchester, with nothing but suitcases full of clothing and $2,000 cash—not counting the Weebles folding garage I carried like a security blanket through the entire trip.

Mum quickly discovered that the reality of being a doctor in Manchester was hardly the royal road to riches. She started all over again, going from consultant to house officer—the bottom rung on the UK medical ladder. She worked dawn to dusk, and then moonlighted as a locum for vacationing doctors. We learned to adapt to her long hours, knowing she was doing what it took to support three kids all by herself, with only minimal help from my grandparents.

Our reliance on her and love for her got an awful fright when Mum slipped and fell down a narrow staircase, landing in a tangled heap. She yelped when I tried to carry her to the couch. We kids ran around hysterically for awhile. Eventually realizing that running around hysterically wasn't doing her any good, we settled down around her and were feeding her grapes as though they were some kind of elixir. Whether it was the fruit or the love, she was no worse for the wear, sporting nothing more than some nasty bruises.

Though I was no more than 9, it was an early, terrifying foreshadowing of life without Mum.

When I was around 8, Grandma died, and we moved into a new development in Heaton Mersey, near Stockport. The new home was an adventurous boy's dream. Behind the backyard lay a building site loaded with piles of timber, bricks, and half-finished shells.

Mum made it clear I could explore only if I didn't stray beyond our street. She had good reason for her concern. My father had sent Granddad a letter threatening to kidnap us and spirit us away to Nigeria, never to be seen again. We knew it was no idle threat, because he did show up now and again, and Mum would sequester us at a friends place while he stayed in the UK.

One day my best friend, Paul, and I strayed from our street, but not outside the neighorhood. When I returned home, Mum was standing in the front of the house alongside a serious-looking police officer with a big dog. She was so distraught that she was shaking. Although we lobbied every day for more freedom, we did not exceed her limits again.

When Dad came to the UK, Mum would somehow learn of his whereabouts. We would be driven to the safe house of one of Mum's friends. Our nights away were scary because we knew Mum would be confronting our dad.

When Dad finally stopped showing up, I was nearly 10. Only then were we allowed to take our bikes around the block, temporarily out of Mum's watchful eye.

By then, Mum's attention had turned to more pressing matters. We barely got by, largely because she was now paying a mortgage and had hired a nanny to look after us while she worked.

Mum worked mornings as a junior physician at a clinic. In the afternoon, she made rounds before returning to the clinic, where she would work through dinner. She also worked part-time at a local psycho-geriatric hospital, Cheadle Royal Hospital.

In those days doctors, at least in England, still made house calls and Mum would bring me along on her Saturday rounds. We'd start at the hospital, where I'd fetch coffee for the doctors and pull files.

When we arrived at a patient's home, Mom sometimes had me wait in the car. Either she didn't want me to risk catching something, or she was shielding me from the trauma of what I might witness.

The only time I can recall her complaining about the incessant demands was on Christmas Day, when she was guaranteed to get at least one call from someone with a stomach ache. She'd come home, grumbling, "Of course you've got stomach pain. You just stuffed an entire turkey in there!"

Mum eventually became a partner in a busy surgical practice. She still shuttled between two jobs, but she finally made a decent living. It was inspiring just watching her take on the world, and the determination she demonstrated rubbed off. Her children have never been afraid of setting goals and letting nothing stop us in the pursuit of them.

Naturally, I was determined to be a doctor when I grew up. But before long I realized I had little interest in physical ailments. I lacked the stomach for blood, guts, and poxes. But I grew fascinated, sitting in all those sad living rooms during Mum's house calls, by how to relieve emotional suffering, especially among children. What I most hoped to emulate was Mum's bedside manner, her ability to serve as an emotional as well as a medical caretaker, to soothe the hurt, no matter how dire.

In the meantime I basked in her reflected glory. "Oh, you must be Dr. Amaechi's son," people would say everywhere I went.

I still swell with pride when someone stops me on the street in England—not to recognize me as the former NBA player, but to regale me with glowing stories about how Mum touched their lives.

CHAPTER 2 ●●●] Invisible Giant

Perhaps subconsciously, I imagined a calling such as being a psychologist would help me come to terms with the unhappier aspects of my own childhood.

By age 10, near the end of primary school, I already stood a head above my classmates at nearly six feet tall. In fact, I was taller than many of my teachers. There was no chance the other kids would catch up.

Not only was I tall; I was brown-skinned and increasingly round. All those scones with clotted cream were adding up. In a school dominated by skinny white kids, I stood out not so much like a sore thumb but a fat one.

Especially in gym. Donning my first uniform—bright red shorts—belly protruding, was an exercise in humiliation, worse even than Granddad's signature haircut. Team photos were posted on the public notice board, enshrining my shame for the entire school.

It chilled my heart to compare myself to my scrawny peers. In that self-absorption of pre-adolescence, I looked high and low for evidence to confirm my fears that I was horribly, horribly different.

Kids being kids, I didn't have to look far. For swimming class, we were bused to the local Victorian baths. Changing rooms ringed the pool. On the drive there, I fixated on the water torture to come. These were the days before baggy board shorts were popular, and everyone donned skimpy Speedos seemingly designed to make all but the most perfect specimens look ridiculous.

As I stood in line waiting for swim to begin, sucking in my stomach and trying to be inconspicuous, I longed for the cover of water—the cover of anything really. The directive, "Get in the water, boys" was music to my ears.

At the saltwater baths during summer camping trips, I'd become a strong swimmer, thanks in part to a mammoth wingspan. When the PE teacher noticed, he had the brilliant idea of staging an underwater swimming competition, basically a pointless exercise to determine who could hold their breath the longest. I'd hoped against hope to be the invisible giant; instead, with my lung capacity, I became the main attraction.

As I approached the finish line, my lungs ached and my arms burned so badly I wasn't even sure I was moving forward. When I surfaced, I expected sure defeat, only to see the teacher's smiling face as he knelt at the side of the pool to congratulate me. I had won. And for a moment, I felt a surge of pride.

Then one of my classmates yelled, "He's supposed to be able to hold his breath; he's a whale!"

It was one of those moments when you swear you can feel a part of yourself die inside. I'd been christened a monster forever. I dunked my head to avoid the rising ridicule.

Whenever I showed up for mandatory swim, I'd be greeted by similar name-calling. And it wasn't just one bully. It seemed everyone joined in the fun. All I could do was force out a pretend laugh, but deep down I had to admit the words cut.

My only recourse was to come up with creative excuses to skip class. There were clearly advantages to having a doctor in the family, and the range of exotic illnesses I came down with surprised my teachers.

The experience in the swim class had lasting psychological ramifications. For my entire adolescence I wouldn't get near a public pool without covering my entire body the instant I emerged from the water. Even today I'm rarely spotted anywhere near a body of water. In fact, the only way to photograph me shirtless is in my own pool or Jacuzzi, surrounded by a privacy fence. I had tan lines for a month from three days spent on Miami Beach in a large white vest. (And that was during my NBA days when I was certainly not the fat, ugly kid.)

Having written the doctor's notes, Mum was aware of my suffering. When I told her about my new nickname, she advised me to ignore it. "People who try to make you feel bad just for the hell of it are peasants," she said. "Stare at these kids and repeat *peasant* in your head. It's like when an idiot calls a genius stupid."

By peasants, she didn't mean poor people. Rather, she meant people with a poverty of spirit. And she was right. I longed to be around people for whom my appearance was irrelevant or, better still, people who thought it was a positive trait.

Only later was I able to put her advice to use. I developed a devastating, withering look that, in combination with my stature, could halt even the worst bullies in their tracks. But at the time I couldn't find a way to turn it to my advantage. The best I could do was take some consolation in my ability to turn the other cheek—a virtue that is meaningless among adolescents.

Only once did I fight back. In primary school I had but one friend, David, who was similarly nerdy only smaller, slight, and pale. We were united as powerless outcasts, so we spent our time together imagining ourselves as various superheroes, destined for glory and the redemption of revenge.

One snowy Stockport fall, a few days before my birthday, we were making a snowman in the school playground when a bunch of kids began pointing, jeering, and pelting us with snowballs. Instinctively, I placed myself between the barrage and my friend, expecting that simple move would put an end to the attack.

When it didn't, I became enraged. I leaped at the kids, lashing out with my legs and arms. I hit nothing but air, but nonetheless managed to scatter the attackers, who raced back to the protective confines of the school.

I walked alone into the school building, and was hanging up my coat when one of my tormenters said, "What you did back there, that was pretty cool." For the rest of that day, I held my head high.

At any rate, my self-consciousness about my body made me want to avoid sports of any kind. I just said no to rope-climb, vaulting, track, even cricket, where players wore uniforms whiter than the snow in Russia. I wanted to wipe the entire subject out of my life.

Why put myself in the position of sticking out for something I detested anyway? I despised exertion of any kind. I hated to sweat. The more strenuous the exercise, the more I loathed it. Even long walks sent me around the bend.

To this day, I've never understood those who enjoy the supposed "high" of intense workouts. To me it is pointless pain and suffering. I've experienced plenty of endorphin surges after an intense workout, but I must say I've had better highs from a cup of Earl Grey tea.

Instead, I came up with a far superior activity to pass the time: sitting in a chair reading, and drinking enough delicious tea to fill a swimming pool.

In secondary school, when I was 11, Mum granted me a book allowance, and I could be spotted browsing in bookstores most days. The rest of the time I was slumped in a cubicle in the library, book positioned strategically over my face. I can still get a comforting feeling from imagining a library's musty smell.

I read and reread every volume in the Hardy Boys series. It never bothered me that every story was identical, save for the setting. Some American terms stumped me. I never could figure out the meaning of the word "jalopy" until I was finally living in the States.

It's no surprise my taste ran to the escapist. There were no social pressures or demands, no put-downs directed at me, and it was always others who felt the sting of hurtful words.

Like a lot of kids, I identified with outcasts who took on great magical powers to overcome their evil tormenters. I devoured *The Lion, the Witch, and the Wardrobe* and Isaac Asimov's *I, Robot*. I was there when the Robots finally broke Asimov's laws, I was the last hero of the noble mercenaries, and I was always a brilliant Hardy Boy, even if I more closely resembled Chet, their chunky but loyal friend.

The massive amount of time I spent with my nose buried in books helps explain why I had few friends. It got so bad that in one class I concentrated so hard on a book I was reading that when the teacher called on me, I didn't answer. When I finally looked up, the entire class was laughing as the teacher waved for my attention.

Not long after the snowball incident, Mum threw me a 10th birthday party. Only one kid showed up. As a reward for my loyalty and protective instinct, David had dumped me, apparently not wanting to associate with the school whale any longer.

Because he was a year younger, he had declared that he needed to "move on," since I would be graduating and he needed to find new friends anyway. I sent him a sorrowful "but we were friends, I trusted you, you lied to me" note. He mailed it back with no comment other than having corrected my spelling mistakes in red ink.

●●•

Along with books, food was my greatest diversion.

On the way to Stockport Grammar School, I'd stop at the sweet shop and fill my pockets with Bon Bons, Pear Drops, Cola Bottles, Gummy Bears, Twix, and Kit Kats.

Not surprisingly, I ballooned further. The bigger I got, the more I needed my candy therapy.

My candy stash did have one advantage: I would offer sweets to kids I hoped to befriend as a sort of bribe. It worked. My 11th birthday party was packed with kids of all sorts.

This was a big boost, especially since I had signed up for a backpacking trip to the Isle of Mull the next year and I needed a tent-mate. I bunked with a boy named Andrew. As soon as we'd assembled our tent, we had an argument and I was left shivering on my own, awakened at 2 a.m. by sheep foraging for food we'd stored under the tent.

I spent the rest of that trip by myself, until one kid couldn't handle his knapsack and a teacher asked me put it on my shoulders, so I was carrying one on my front, one on back. I spent the rest of the trip as a pack mule, struggling up boggy hills with an increasingly heavy load.

My English teacher cooed that I was generous and kind; I just felt like an ass.

●••

By secondary school at 12, sports became mandatory. I carefully chose a sport I'd never heard of, lacrosse, confident I'd be so bad that I wouldn't have to play much. Figuring that if nothing else, my size would make it hard to get around me, the teacher placed me in goal. We played in the frigid Manchester winter, a crust of frost turning the muddy fields as hard as concrete.

In the cold, the solid rubber ball, hurtling at me in excess of 100 miles per hour, felt like a rock and stung like a swarm of wasps. As a massive target in a small net, there were times when I wondered whether players were having more fun pelting my body with the ball than actually figuring out how to get it past me.

As the season came to an end, I figured I'd bumbled and stumbled my way out of competitive sports forever. Once again the PE teachers had other ideas, and I was ordered to take up rugby, an even more brutal sport that also necessitated running rather than standing in front of a net. I didn't so much fear getting hurt; I feared hurting someone else.

During one practice the coach, Mr. Shackelton, ordered me to demonstrate a flying tackle I'd recently performed by accident when I tripped over a scrawny kid half my size. When I refused, coach threw a mini-tantrum. From that day on, I never had a tolerance for "screamer" coaches.

During one game, I remember I was dutifully pulling kids out of the ruck, tossing them around like potato sacks, when I heard the father of a player on the other side scream, "Get that fuckin' mutant freak out of there!"

Mum, taking in the game from the sidelines, did not take kindly to a verbal attack on her only son. From a distance I saw her approach the offending father. She spoke politely through barely contained rage. Whatever she said, it had an impact. The man was not present on the sidelines when the game ended—or ever again.

I have no memory of who won the game, or even how I played, but I grinned approvingly at my hero all the way home, shaking my head at her toughness.

My play remained atrocious. But it did, much like the candy bribery years earlier, improve my social life. When I was nearly 16, after three seasons of lacrosse, I joined the fifth-year team, We took a road trip to Newcastle, 300 miles northeast. I shared a tiny hotel room with three other kids, one of whom, Peter Carroll, would become my best friend.

All the social experiences that had eluded me became clear, mostly through Peter's gregariousness. It helped that our team went undefeated. For the first time, I could see the potential fun in sports—even if I never did get my jollies from two hours drenched in sweat and mud, mashed up against miscreants half my bulk.

Peter was not repulsed by my mutant freakishness. In fact, we suddenly saw that we could exploit it to our full advantage. My height also meant I could buy beer more easily than anyone else.

Where athletics failed me, academics made me. I may have been physically loathsome, but with enough reading I figured at least I could be more clever than everyone else. It was my last hope to be exceptional at something, anything, to become an intellectual superhero.

In the UK, students are streamed according to a series of rigorous exams. At age 12, I was devastated to end up in 2L, which I considered the smartest of the dumb bunch. (Peter was in the top stream.) At 16, we are faced with the O-levels, a series of atrocious eight-hour exams covering everything we'd been taught over the first five years of secondary school.

I locked myself in my room, studying around the clock. I may have run from competition on the playing field, but when it came to academics I went for the jugular. In primary school I'd kept a secret list, updated weekly, ranking my competition. Now was my chance to make Mum proud and prove I was no stupid giant.

The results were distributed in an envelope. Mum picked me up in her red Volvo, and we parked away from the school gates for some privacy. My heart was pounding as I peeked at my scores.

Five A's, three B's.

Fat *and* dumb. Over and over, I berated myself before bursting into tears.

This meant plenty of kids were smarter. My own ranking system had been turned upside down. Now that someone else did the measuring, my ranking system all those years seemed fraudulent.

"John, you don't understand," Mum said in her best consoling voice. "You did better than most of the rest of the kids your age in the country. You should be proud."

That night I hung out with Peter. He had scored straight A's. I was happy for him, but of course, it didn't make the blow any easier.

Luckily his parents, doctors themselves, were bohemian compared to Mum, who wouldn't let her kids go beyond a glass or two of wine. It was from the Carrolls that I learned the advantages of tippling, especially after what I was convinced was one of the worst days of my life.

Over a nice meal at a fancy restaurant, I lamented my scores. I ordered a black Russian. Back at their place, I helped myself to beer from the cupboard until I was bladdered, and Peter and I stayed up late carrying on. Even though I woke up the next morning with a fierce hangover, I felt better. Sharing my woes with a friend—a relatively new experience—was strangely comforting.

It was the beginning of a long friendship, forged over beer and a kaleidoscope of other alcoholic beverages. The drinking age was 18, but what merchant was going to ask for identification from someone who was six-foot-eight?

●●●

There's nothing like the attention of a pretty girl to make an adolescent boy feel better about himself. Peter asked me whether I fancied Amber, a beauty of a classmate. Since we were the only two brown-skinned people at school, my new friends must have thought it was a brilliant match. On an aesthetic level, I could see she was attractive, gorgeous even, and I'll admit the idea of going out with her made my heart flutter.

I agreed to a double date with another friend, Tom, and his girlfriend, Helen. I bought a new outfit, baggy jeans (decidedly uncool in '90s Britain) and an even baggier T-shirt for the big night out. As I stood in front of the mirror, scrutinizing my outfit, I noticed sweat dampening my new clothes.

Even though I was far more confident than I had been just a few years earlier, I was still pretty awkward. It was hard to believe I had *any* friends, let alone a *girl*friend.

We had a drink at the bar at the Davenport Theatre and then took our seats at the cinema. I was so nervous I stared at the screen but saw nothing. About half way into the movie, I could tell I was supposed to do something. Amber eyed me as if to say, *What the hell are you waiting for?*

It was as if I was living one of those romantic scenes that exist only in the movies, watching myself from afar as I carefully snaked my long arm around her shoulder. She snuggled up to me, and I leaned down for my first smooch.

Rockets did not go off. Instead, the sound of our teeth clanging seemed to ring around the entire cinema. The next day's "let's just be friends" phone call seemed all too predictable.

As an adult, it took me a long time to believe my friends' tales of adolescent erotic adventures. Sitting next to Amber in that movie theater, sexuality was a bigger mystery than any Hardy Boys caper. While the older schoolboys bragged about their exploits, about the girls they were supposedly "nailing," I hid in the library, lost in science fiction and fantasy. In some ways I was precocious. Sexually, I was way behind.

The first glimmer that I might be *really* different came around age 15. We were forced into a torture scheme known as the mile run, in which we sprinted around the track for as long as we could stay on our feet. Mum's notes had stopped getting me excused at this point—I suffered from the boy-who-got-out-of-gym-one-too-many-times-syndrome—and I actually had to participate.

Public showering was and is not high on my list of favorite activities. I preferred to head to my next period, sweat pouring off my clothing and onto the classroom floor, to the humiliation of undressing in public.

That day I was assigned the role of shower monitor. Since I was not fit to run, the teacher probably figured it was the least I could do. The post entailed standing just outside the shower room while everyone washed and checking to make sure that the locker room was empty by the end of the period and that no one had left their belongings behind.

In front of my eyes went procession of young men, clad only in underwear, and for some reason that was lost on me, it was an exhilarating sight. I forced my gaze to stay above their waists.

I didn't fancy anyone in particular; it was a generalized kind of eroticism kids feel at that age. As far as I was concerned, it didn't add up to homosexuality—a word that had no meaning for me at the time. I barely knew "those kind of people" existed. Until the terrible advent of AIDS, they were truly the invisible minority. I heard the occasional reference to "poofs," usually from sixth formers, the oldest students. (Brits had, at that time, much less creative anti-gay epithets.) But the insults were never directed at me. No one ever dared accuse the biggest guy in the room of being a fag.

CHAPTER 3 ●●●] The Game

Not long after my 17th birthday, I was walking down Market Street toward the Arndale Centre, a yellow 1970s shopping center that makes hideous American malls look attractive.

At six-foot-eight, I was still two inches from my full adult height. At that size, you get plenty of stares. People come up to you and say brilliant things like, "You're tall!" or, "How's the air up there?" I tried to be polite, but inane remarks like that get boring fast.

On this day, however, two middle-aged men stopped me to say something a bit more interesting. They introduced themselves as coaches, then politely inquired whether "I'd like to try basketball," *try* being the operative word. Since I was clearly in abysmal shape, stomach protruding under my tent-like shirt, they correctly assumed I didn't play.

I don't know why I agreed, especially given my well-known antipathy for physical activity of any sort. I suppose it was a chance to escape the brutality that was rugby, where I was little more than an obvious target.

Knowing next to nothing about basketball meant I could approach it with an open mind. One of the few things I knew about the game was that being tall was not only good but great. I imagined, for once, being surrounded by other big people, ordinary rather than freakish. Perhaps I'd finally stumbled across a sport I could actually enjoy, a sport where a shy young man could shine.

A few weeks later, there was a message for me at school from Dave McLean, a representative of Shop Local, a basketball club named after its sponsor, a grocery store that paid 50 pounds to plaster its name across the uniforms. I was told the team played at a community center in Chorlton, which turned out to be next to the cemetery where my grandmother's ashes were interned.

The location was the first test of my resolve. To get there, I would need to walk a mile, wait for the bus, then make another connection. The whole trip took an hour each way.

Which would cut way into my reading and tea time.

It was a tiny gym with a ceramic tile floor. I didn't realize it then, but basketball courts are *not* made of clay. Asking a guy to play on anything other than wood, at least indoors, is like asking a ballet dancer to perform on concrete.

The backboard and basket were fixed to the wall, making lay-ups treacherous. Players complained of twisted ankles as they banged off the wall while leaping for the hoop.

I'd seen American basketball on late-night television, but I barely knew the rules. Brits think of basketball the way Americans think of cricket: a bizarre game played *over there.* (Sometimes I wondered what would have happened if we had stayed in Boston. With the cult-like popularity of the Celtics, I might have taken up the game much earlier.)

It didn't take me long to understand a game that made rugby and lacrosse look complicated. However, playing it was another matter entirely. Playing it with the kind of power and finesse I witnessed on TV seemed downright impossible.

Once again, I was atrocious. I showed absolutely no natural talent. I was awkward, out of shape, and slow. I had no touch; my ball-handling was nonexistent, my footwork clumsy. I was more likely to trip than to score. I was a hacking hazard to the safety of my frightened teammates.

I warned the other players, most of whom were older and far more experienced, that even though I may have looked like I belonged on a basketball court, I'd never actually been on one. And it wasn't like I was some large, brown version of Roy Hobbs, some sort of natural. To the contrary, I was flat-out terrible at *every* sport. *Natural ability* was a concept God had made up to torture me.

Despite my physical awkwardness, it was clear I'd found a home on the court. There was no talk of whales or mutant freaks. I'd gone from people complaining that I was crap to being lauded for my potential. Someone other than my family saw me as special.

When sides were chosen, to my shock I was picked first, solely on the basis of my height. I figured the least I could do was reward such faith with my best efforts.

The other players and our coach, Dave Smith, were eager to share their wisdom; they saw me as their project, someone who could be molded into something special. They wanted me to be great so the team could be greater.

Even so, I can't say I fell in love with the game right then; it was still exercise, after all. In some ways I would rather have been lounging on the couch at home, reading and listening to Erasure on my headphones.

What I enjoyed was not so much the sport of it, but the sense of accomplishment and the accolades, which came from every direction with even the slightest hint of improvement. Mum approved of my eager participation, Dave my intense desire to learn, my teammates my nascent ability to change shots, literally just by standing in the paint with my arms held over my head when a shot went up.

The reason I recall the first shot I sank in a league game—a hook shot in the lane—was not the art of it. It was because of the resounding cheers coming from the sidelines and the high-fives from my teammates.

●●●

Today Manchester United is renowned for English football (soccer to you Americans). But back then it featured a crack basketball team, too.

After three months with Shop Local, I'd made enough strides (based primarily on my size, truth be told) to earn notice in the small world of British basketball.

Joe Forber, the closest thing to a British basketball legend, lured me away to United. Joe saw in me not just an unusually big young man, but a big young man who had begun to develop soft hands, quickness around the hoop, and even some game savvy—qualities I never imagined possessing.

It helped that United had teams that played at all levels—the senior team in top European competition and the best junior and cadet teams. I'd be playing with the most talented young players, a better test of my ability.

Six months after I joined, we competed for the junior championship at the historic Royal Albert Hall in Central London. They laid the most lustrous hardwood floor I'd ever seen in a spectacular venue that had seen royal command performances of opera, ballet, and theater. The vaulted ceilings shone with gold and claret red. As I looked around, I was in awe of the expanse of seats; the idea of playing in front of thousands of people was mortifying.

I played all of two minutes—which may explain why we won the title—sprinting up and down the court a few times. I think I would have fainted from panic had anyone actually passed me the ball.

From the bench I soaked in the atmosphere: legions of cheering fans, the ferocity of competition, the creativity of acrobatic plays. The experience gave me a taste of the thrills to come—if only I could get my game together.

Joe was determined to make that happen. He saw my promise better than I, lost in the endless struggle to improve, ever could. He kept repeating that I could go far. Frankly, I was satisfied with an unfamiliar sensation, the simple joy of blending into the crowd. At that point I wasn't ready to risk being a standout.

But I vowed to follow Joe wherever he could lead me. The silent type, he rarely let on what he was thinking. Since he rarely seemed upset, I was always wary of what would happen if he were ever to go off. Imagine Bobby Knight without the bombast. (Not easy, I know.)

At one of our first practices he taught the dreaded backboard drill. The players form a line. The first guy throws the ball off the board and each subsequent player follows up bouncing it off the board without letting it hit the floor. As we looped around a folding chair, Joe would pull it farther and farther from the backboard.

Just when it seemed impossible to keep up, he'd pull a player out, stepping up the pace even more. Try doing that for 20 minutes without a break, especially when you are the kind of athlete whose size-15 shoes are practically cemented to the floor.

It was after several months of this and other drills—and the general rigor of Joe's practices—that I noticed I was shedding pounds. The whale was rounding into, perhaps not quite a porpoise, but, well, a killer whale. Still large but leaner and more aggressive. I even rediscovered my belly button.

Since stamina became a matter of court survival, I paid a more attention to my diet. Though I never lost my hankering for sweets, I was able to resist more than indulge.

Without realizing it, I was adopting a whole new identity, one based much less on outsider status, on victimization. I'd found a place where I could be myself—whatever I chose that to be.

Joe was the mentor I'd never had and always desired. In many ways, he was the first positive male role model in my life. His patience, his perseverance, his willingness to teach and to lead— all of these became qualities that I would try to make a part of my life.

Joe would drive me back and forth to practice. Because we lacked a regular gym, moving around the area like itinerant farm workers, this was of no small significance. But he never drove to my house, always picking a prearranged spot. I took this to be a subtle suggestion that nothing was free, that I would have to meet him half-way. He could guide me, but the hard work was on me.

Under Joe's tutelage, I made steady progress. I learned to box out, timing my leaps for rebounds. It turned out that Joe had been right: I had soft hands and could catch the ball near the hoop, make a clean move, and spin it deftly home.

I was not yet a significant performer, getting only limited minutes. Joe was not going to treat me as his pet. I was going to have to earn a spot in the rotation. The gains I made had to come in our gruelling practices, three days a week.

He broke down the game into component parts. "Basics before skills," he always said. In other words, getting footwork down was more essential than actually making shots. Deft positioning through proper technique, Joe knew, would lead to balance and good shots. He taught me to fill the lanes on the break at precisely the right angle, to let the ball slide gently off my fingertips when I shot—all before I could actually pull any of these things off with consistency.

The best players, even in the basketball-starved UK, had started years before their voices broke, putting me at least a decade behind. In fact, many players had already spent more time in competition that I would in an entire career, no matter how long I played.

But I had the Joe Forber advantage: learning the fundamentals *before* developing the bad habits. Joe found himself trying to get players to discard the bad as often as he was teaching the good. Even though I made lots of mistakes, I was going to learn to play the right way or not at all.

While I had loads of support, I noted the corollary effect: Plenty of people took a perverse glee in informing me that at 17 I was not only too old but also not nearly talented enough. "You started too late and you are not athletic enough to make up for it," was how one veteran British player put it. Others insisted I was too slow or too uncoordinated. Still others in the sports establishment said it didn't matter anyway. Basketball was not a British sport.

At first, such negativity stung. Although these people were only were assessing my skills and not me as a human being, it felt deeply personal in a way I didn't fully comprehend.

But I gradually learned to transform the nay-saying into an advantage. Who were they to tell me what I could do—or could not? As Joe reminded me, only *I* could determine the outcome.

While much of the criticism was technically accurate, it missed the point. My lack of skill was hardly the determining factor in whether I would succeed. What mattered was how well I learned my limits and improved on my strengths. I was determined to use the skills I did have to overcome the ones I didn't.

Why is it that some of the best players don't necessarily have the best physical skills? They have something ineffable, an ability to make everyone around them better, to bear down at just the right moment in the game.

These players know the key to solid ball: It's not about *them;* It's about the team.

CHAPTER 4 ••] The Guillotine

After that first season with United, I traveled to Anglesey, an island off Wales, on a school biology field trip. It was right before Christmas break, and we were there to study the rich natural history of wildlife and flora in Charles Darwin's path.

On our final night there, I returned to the chalet with three other students. In a hurry to get in from the cold, I somehow managed to put my right hand directly through the substandard plate glass door. I couldn't stop my arm until the glass reached my elbow. Remembering random advice from my Mum about avoiding extra damage in these situations, I tried to pull my arm out slowly. At that point, I had one small cut on my forearm.

At first, I thought I was the luckiest guy in the world. But when I got my arm out up to my wrist, the putty holding the glass in place collapsed and the entire top plate dropped, guillotining my hand. Every tendon and nerve was severed; my wrist hung by a bone to my forearm. Everything was bathed in a dark shade of crimson—my classmates, my clothing, the floor, the white walls.

There's nothing more sickening than looking down to see and feel your own blood rushing out of your body. My heartbeat, usually pushing my blood through my veins, was now simply draining my body of its life force.

I stared at my right hand for a moment, fingers limp and cold, before grabbing it with my left hand and pulling the pieces together to keep the arm in one piece and staunch the blood flow.

I'd seen my mother in action long enough to know what to do. Wrapping a towel tightly around my wrist, I elevated my arm as I raced to the teacher's chalet, where I found my favorite biology teacher, Mr. Gregg, who got me into the back of his Peugeot. Lying face up, arm pointing to the roof, we raced 50 miles to the closest emergency room.

As I faded in and out of consciousness, blood dripped into my eyes and mouth. Mr. Gregg encouraged me to talk all the way there, both to keep me conscious and to distract me from the agony.

When we reached the ambulance bay, a nurse looked down at me on the stretcher and declared, "You're a big lad!"

No kidding.

Even at death's door, I couldn't escape people's stupidity.

"So what do you do?" she then asked.

I spat blood. Through reddened teeth I said, "I *used* to play basketball."

Looking back, the comment surprises me. It shows how seriously I was taking the game, even though I'd started less than a year ago.

A junior physician wanted to sew up the main artery right away, but I knew that stopping the blood supply entirely would not be a good thing for the future of my hand. So instead, I spent that night with a blood pressure cuff strapped around my arm.

The pain felt like a thousand tiny razor blades. The constant view of my wrist attached to my arm by gauze did not help matters much. Despite my writhing agony, the staff refused, for medical reasons unbeknownst to me, to provide adequate pain medication.

My life was no longer in danger, but as I lay in my hospital bed, I grew depressed about the reality that I could not feel or move my hand from the wrist to the fingers. It was hard to get my mind around the idea that I'd lost control of the most dextrous parts of my body.

In the morning, a consultant with expertise in these kinds of injuries stopped by my bed to check out the damage. He wanted to know whether I'd tried to kill myself. It was so obviously an accident, the most unwelcome one possible, that I simply grimaced.

He released the pressure from the cuff, which immediately showered the junior doctor next to him with blood. He tried to be reassuring, but I read the truth in his face: "My God, the poor kid's going to lose his hand."

I'd avoided calling Mum at first because I didn't want to traumatize her in the middle of the night. Far too many patients had done that already. But rather than seeing my gesture for what it was, when she finally found out, she was beside herself. I hadn't seen her this angry since I strayed from her block limits back when Dad was threatening to kidnap us.

She wanted to be by my side, directing my medical care, from the outset. Now she had an ambulance drive the hundred miles from North Wales to Withington Hospital in Manchester, where she met me at the door.

Through her contacts, she located a renowned specialist in microsurgery, at the time a relatively new field. The grafting surgery I needed had been done successfully only once, she discovered—on a Green Beret who'd injured his hand in combat. During the six-hour operation, the surgeon reattached dozens of ligaments and nerves in the hope that I would eventually regain a full range of motion.

I woke up in Manchester the next day feeling numb, drugged to the eyeballs. Mum handed me a sweet "get well soon" card from my schoolmates. But all I could do was stare at my dead hand, now wrapped in a plaster cast, wondering how anyone gets well from this.

The state of shock was such that I don't remember all the things I must have done while recuperating: watching TV, drinking tea, talking on the phone. Mum, my sisters, and Mum's friend Auntie Nell doted on me. And my friends, especially Peter, came around for cheer-up visits.

When I finally went back to school after missing a month, it was hard to concentrate and even harder to take notes with my left hand. The material just washed over me. At the end of that Stockport Grammar School year, the headmaster's report read: "John must stop using his hand as a psychological crutch."

I'd yet to regain any feeling in my right hand, had spent eight weeks in a cast (six more in a suspension device that made me look like an android), and still couldn't write properly. Yet my hand, damaged on a school trip, somehow had become not a horrible injury but a bad excuse.

The headmaster's cruel words finished me with school, and I made no great efforts to attend for the rest of sixth form.

Since Mum left the house early every morning, she was not aware of the extent to which I was playing hooky. When I bothered, which was not often, I went to school in the afternoon.

I managed to complete my A-levels anyway. Mum's concern when she saw my grades was that I was putting myself in a position where it would be hard to get into a top college.

She was right. I needed to refocus on school work. But first I had to get myself back on the court.

●●•

Whatever the long-term outcome of the operation, the surgeon warned that my newfound athletic career likely was doomed. I fell into the depths of a depression so severe that Mum had to drag me out of bed. The new life I'd created for myself had been ended in the time it takes for glass to slice flesh.

Mum tried her best to reassure me, pointing out that I had a great support system and lots to look forward to, even if the surgery wasn't completely successful. She reminded me that as long as my schoolwork didn't slip any further, I would still have my choice of universities and professions.

But all I could do was imagine what the doctors termed the results of failed surgery—a "claw hand" protruding from my mutant body. I would go from fitting in, even being welcomed, to being a freak again.

The hardest part to accept was that I had just starting to make headway. Instead of disappearing into the corner of the library, I was standing tall in the middle of a basketball court and announcing my presence. The gains I'd made were only secondarily on the court. The main progress was in the vastly more complicated psychological terrain of self-esteem.

After feeling sorry for myself, my surgeon and my mother ganged up on me to start rehab work. Once the cast came off in a few months, there would be plenty of exercises for my hand. The problem was that I had no idea how to restart basketball workouts carrying a heavy cast. Basketball, after all, is a game of hands. Your feet get you into position, but your hands finish the job.

Then I hit upon a plan: My right hand may have been in a plaster cast, but I still had a working left.

Barely. Like most young ball players, I had not paid much attention to what players call their "weak hand," which was now going to have to serve as my "strong hand."

I spent hours dribbling, shooting, passing, and defending with my left. (I had to refrain from rebounding, which generally can't be done with one hand unless your name happens to be Shaquille.) Since I had hardly begun to master my natural side, I felt more pathetic than ever.

As usual, Joe was there. We would break into an empty gym somewhere and, while he urged me on, I'd run the Mikan drill, one-handed, dribbling up and down the court, over and over again, cupping the ball with my left hand and gently laying it in.

At first the ball bounced away, banged off my foot, or clanged against the rim. It felt like learning to drive on the opposite side of the road.

Joe told me years later that my demeanor was so surly, my attitude so negative, that it was one of the least enjoyable coaching experiences of his long career. I am eternally grateful he stuck around, instilling a permanent lesson in never giving up on even the most petulant youngsters. I learned that there is potential in the darkest of characters—an insight that would prove crucial later in my life.

Sure enough, after several months of hard work, I gradually gained a semblance of control over my left hand—and the ball— to the point where it was almost as solid as my rather shaky right had once been.

My mood lifted, until it came time for the doctor to cut off the cast. With no muscle tone, my forearm had withered practically to the bone. It was half the size of my left arm. When I got into a warm bath at home, eight months of dead skin sloughed off like a snake's skin. Waves of discouragement washed over me.

I had been using my left hand to get through the day. Now I had to relearn even the simplest muscle movements with the injured one. Activities I had taken for granted—picking up a pen, turning the page of a book, pouring a cup of tea (a big deal for an Englishman)—were treacherous, both physically and emotionally.

It terrified me when I realized the hand, now seemingly outside my body, was numb. I could lay my hand on top of the stove flame and feel nothing at all—a neat party trick perhaps, but hardly something I could live with.

The medical priority was to stop adhesions from forming. I worked with a medieval torture device that stretches the hand and fingers by creating resistance with heavy elastic bands. After a few weeks of pain, I started to regain limited movement and strength in my right hand. But it was still unclear how complete a recovery I could make.

I was eager to try my rebuilt hand in competition. Once I regained some muscle memory, I made tentative forays. I started out by going to an outdoor court in Stretford and shooting free throws. Since I had no feeling in the hand, I had no touch—the basis of all shooting and passing. The ball got nowhere near the hoop. The word *swish* had lost its appeal.

I tried a more direct route. I got a running start and dunked. As my right hand hit the steel rim on the way down, it exploded in pain so intense that a burst of light went off in my eyes. I fell to the concrete in a heap, writhing. Fortunately, the bones withstood the blow. And the pain meant that I was getting some feeling back.

A few weeks later, I tried playing tennis with Peter, figuring swinging a racket was less stressful than dunking a basketball. I picked up a racket and practiced swinging freely. My grip felt fine.

But when I actually made contact with the ball, the racket clanged to the ground like a hot potato. I walked off the court, shaking my head, as Peter chased me, vainly sputtering words of consolation.

To make matters worse, I had to find a new team. Joe had quit as coach of United, frustrated by the routine hardships of English basketball: lack of funding; second-rate, far-flung facilities; the difficulty of keeping players who couldn't afford their own travel or preferred more marketable sports.

My only option was the Chester Jets in Ellesmere Port, 60 miles from home. With two train connections and a bus, it took me nearly two hours to get to practice. Several United players joined me, but the commute forced out many.

On the weekends, the team provided a room at Ellesmere's Penguin Hotel so I could focus on training. We'd practice on Fridays and play on Saturday afternoons. Mum would come to the games and then drive me home, making her one of England's first basketball moms.

To my surprise, my touch was gradually returning. After a month or so, I was pretty much back where I'd been before the injury, or perhaps even better. But still not exactly Dr. J.

Then a funny thing had happened. Not only had I regained the use of my right hand. Now my left was equally strong, or perhaps even stronger. My hands had reversed. My strong hand was now my weak, and vice versa.

What had begun as a devastating injury had somehow become a major basketball advantage. It made me functionally ambidextrous, a huge and rare ability. In a game in which even the most talented players have pronounced tendencies, allowing defenders to shade them one direction or another, I no longer did.

Before long, I'd established myself as one of the best players on the Jets, taking on a leadership role. And it wasn't even because I was the tallest. The Jets drew from a large area, and two players were taller than me. It was because, for the first time, I was actually pretty damned good.

●••

It was in Ellesmere that I met Suzie. We were introduced by a member of the team. She lived nearby, and I spent postgame Friday evenings with her. It was great to have someone other than my teammates to spend time with, especially because, as an athlete herself, she could appreciate the intensity of my aspirations.

Her parents were supportive of our romance. They would retire to their bedroom, leaving us some privacy in the living room. Since it was a public room, there was not *too much* privacy.

One night we lay on the floor watching my favorite TV show, *Star Trek*. When I got up to say goodnight and return to my hotel room, she kissed me. As our lips locked, I practically knocked her over.

Gosh, I'm a lousy kisser, I thought.

I now know that I was merely a lousy heterosexual.

Suzie was fabulous and I enjoyed being around her. But after a while I noticed something was, well, off. Not about her, but about my attraction to her. When we kissed, I'd close my eyes and suddenly one of my teammates appeared in her place, like he'd been beamed into my brain as a joke.

As Freud would say, there is no such thing as a joke, especially when it comes to sex.

The whole thing was disconcerting. But as a teen discovering sexuality, I had no idea what was supposed to be normal. The only thing I knew for sure was that such erotic images were not to be discussed with anyone. Not even my own mother.

The combination of a pretty girlfriend and bursts of dominance on the court lifted my spirits. I spent a lot of extra time at the outdoor courts at Fog Lane Park, where I was king of pick-up ball.

We played with a white-and-green Celtics' basketball, and I was an unstoppable scoring and shot-blocking machine. After overcoming so many hardships, I felt I had earned bragging rights.

One day I was dominating some locals when I proclaimed, to no one in particular, "Some day I'm gonna play in the NBA."

I'm not usually boastful, especially about such a dubious proposition. I'd only been playing for a little more than a year in total—interrupted for nearly nine months by my hand injury—but I was so thrilled to be back on the court, with nearly full use of my hand, that my egotistical enthusiasm got the best of me.

Frankly, it was mostly a challenge to myself. I'd been staying up late, watching American basketball on Channel 4. I was transfixed by the classic Lakers-Celtics battles of the 1980s. I read everything I could about Bird and Magic. Watching these graceful giants bringing down the house, I just knew the NBA was where I belonged, even though my skills were so far from those greats that it was laughable.

"It's a long way from Fog Lane to the NBA," one kid shot back.

He was right. I hadn't the slightest idea how one made it *over there* or whether I'd ever be nearly good enough. It was as fanciful as the plot of an Isaac Asimov novel.

Dribbling the ball through his legs, I dunked over the kid with authority. This time there was no pain, only a surging sense of power.

It was better to let my actions do the talking.

CHAPTER 5 ●●●] Soul in the Dark

Not long after my play blossomed, I was sitting alone in my room, blasting Sting's "They Dance Alone" on the new tower stereo system Mum had bought me. I'm not sure whether it was Sting's beautiful voice or simply the pride of being an integral part of a team, but I had a clarity of purpose like nothing I'd ever felt. And that was saying something, because I'd never exactly been lacking in direction.

Turning off the stereo, I walked into Mum's darkened bedroom, where she was lying on the bed listening, as usual, to a play on BBC Radio 4.

I sat on the edge of her bed. Mum had long envisioned me attending one of the top British colleges, perhaps becoming a doctor, so I wasn't quite sure how she'd react to what I had to say. I told her I wasn't sure where I wanted to go to university.

"There's plenty of choices," she said, and then begun ticking off British schools in London, Leeds, Liverpool, Manchester.

"Actually, I don't know in which *country* I should attend university," I responded.

Then I laid my cards on the table.

"Mum, I want to play in the National Basketball Association, and you have to be in America for that."

"That sounds like a very difficult path," she said matter-of-factly. "One that will take a great deal of effort and planning."

Mum had followed her own long and winding road, albeit for very different reasons, so we shared an unspoken assumption that anything was possible. Even so, I was surprised that she didn't balk at my utterly improbable plan.

Instead, she calmly asked me to write down exactly how I envisioned it happening, perhaps thinking the complexity of the challenge would dissuade me once I looked it in the face.

Or, as I believe now, she truly had faith in me.

For even the most promising American players, making it to the NBA is the ultimate crapshoot. With 13 spots on each of 30 teams, opportunity is as limited as it is competitive.

We were also acutely aware that few Brits had ever made it. At the age of 17 in a game when careers rarely last much into your 30s, my time was running short.

But I didn't waste my energy handicapping my chances. I never saw it as the equivalent of climbing Mount Everest. That would have discouraged me. I was too busy establishing a base camp that would make a run at the peak possible. I was approaching six-foot-ten, so I didn't have to climb the North Face. But on the other hand, I had only a few years to accomplish what American boys did in two decades. And I had to cross an ocean just to start my ascent.

Mum took me seriously enough to start preparing me for my departure. She bought books and maps about the United States, and she stepped up the cooking lessons she was giving me.

Sunday was family time. It was the day the three of us would help Mum prepare a week's worth of meals, which would then be frozen for nights she worked late. Mum's taste was British traditional. She favored shepherd's pie, roasts, steak and kidney pudding, curry, and beef stew. She threw in a few Italian meals— lasagne and spaghetti Bolognese. Since she prepared the week's worth of meals in advance, by noon the house was filled with a mixture of enticing aromas, and we'd eagerly sample each dish.

Duties rotated. One week I'd be responsible for washing and drying dishes, Muriel for slicing and dicing the fresh vegetables and meat, Uki for setting the table.

When I announced my plan, Mum had me study how she prepared dinner. At one point, she laid out the ingredients, declaring that the meal had to be ready in 40 minutes. It would not be long, she knew, before I was fending for myself.

I was so excited about my goal that I stayed up late scribbling in a notebook. Over the next few months, the lined paper over-flowed and became The Plan.

There were sections about my playing characteristics ("goes both ways") and what I must improve upon ("defense" and "rebounding").

Locating the right college program was critical. Joe had long believed that a British NBA star would help catapult our basket-ball to respectability. He explained that the usual route to the pros was through an American college. After all, this was years before it was routine for foreigners to sign directly with American teams, bypassing college. And those players generally come from countries with great or developing basketball pedigrees, something Britain still seriously lacks.

I could have enrolled in an American college, but would not have been able to nail down a scholarship at such a late date. After all, to Americans I was an unknown entity. And we lacked the resources to pay out-of-country tuition. Joe and Mum agreed it would be better to be groomed at an American high school first, that it would be a better adjustment to my new life.

So my first goal had to be finding a high school that could deal with a six-foot-ten Brit with a shallow learning curve. I wrote to the Fulbright program for information on American high schools. Mum insisted the academics be first rate.

The Plan listed the qualities we were looking for in high school and college coaches and mentors generally. Not surprisingly, they closely paralleled Joe's—the ability to both serve as a role model and to groom my game without resorting to negative motivational techniques I already abhorred. There are certain people in life who have a wisdom and nobility that inspires others, from Martin and Coretta Scott King to Mahatma Gandhi. But we also come across such remarkable people in everyday life, people who can have a more personal impact. They are to be sought out and, once found, treasured.

On a more practical level, I mailed what might be called a reverse recruiting letter to several dozen high schools, along the lines of: "Is your school interested in a six-foot-ten British basketball player who also has good grades?"

I got a batch of responses, and Mum narrowed it down to three she thought suitable for a visit.

●●●

At first The Plan was all about basketball. I wrote endlessly about the physical and mental challenges that lay ahead. Then Mum posed a question:

"Son, would you recognize your soul in the dark?"

I didn't get it.

I was frustrated, in the way only the young can be, that she was cryptic and provocative when I was laying out a clear path. The Plan basically had straight arrows running from high school to college to the NBA draft to the pros. Mom had just inserted a zigzag.

I didn't want to have to deal with ethical problems, such as why it is wrong to stomp on other people to get to the top. Or why you were supposed to help others along the way.

"To know where you are going, you must know who you are," she said.

It was Mum at her Zen-like best. I spent hours in the dark silence of my room pondering, waiting fruitlessly for my "soul" to arrive.

Over the years, I have come to understand what she was getting at. She meant I was not John, the six-foot-ten, brown-skinned, English basketball player. I was not defined by the quality of my game, whether I reached my goal, or the number of homes I owned. She was asking simply: Stripped of your physical, material, and social likeness, who are you on the inside, really? What is your essence? Not how others recognize you, superficially. How do you recognize yourself? What is your true identity?

The answer I eventually came up with was to imbue The Plan with my sense of values. After all, I was hardly embarking upon a ruthless, mercenary quest to cash in on the pot of gold at the end of the NBA rainbow.

As the furthest thing from a sports fan, I had only a dim awareness of the wealth and fame awaiting ballplayers, anyway. It was more about proving my worth to myself and to the doubters. Demonstrating that I could achieve my goals, that my word was good. By shining on the stage of the greatest show, I would prove once and for all I was not a pathetic freak.

Thus, The Plan had to be understood in such a way that the people I respected most would not just approve but applaud, and that would allow *me* to be proud of *me*. Recognizing your soul in the dark isn't about becoming a nice person, although that is certainly a worthy a by-product. Rather, it's about truly understanding yourself, your place, your potential as well as your limits.

My goal was not only an extreme physical and emotional challenge, the hardest one I could devise short of being prime minister. It was also a moral one: I had to conduct myself in a way that was consistent with the ideals I'd been brought up with. Identifying and applying them would be as important as, say, improving my rebounding.

Great plans are like sycamores. When the elegant trees reach their apex, they drop seeds that gently swirl to the ground a fair distance from the original trunk. On so many trees, the fruit falls, but they can't take seed because they land in the shadow of their creator's greatness. They simply lie on the ground and rot.

How many times do hear about young NBA players who, having earned millions and achieved stardom, have nothing left to give? Why are so few players prominent—let alone eminent—after they retire?

In the unlikely event that I achieved my goal, it would only be the beginning, not the end. If I did not achieve my goal, The Plan would form the basis of other pursuits.

Nearly two decades later, making the rounds of the inspirational speaking circuit for my company, Animus Consulting, I was able to boil all this ephemeral stuff about the soul in the dark into something more easily comprehensible, something I could share with others. I call it The Eleven Rungs.

1. Hopes, wishes, and dreams are mission statements from the heart.
2. Know yourself: Recognize your soul in the dark.
3. Specificity in word, deed, and plan.
4. Patience, diligence, and honesty.
5. Embrace boldness and assert yourself.
6. Tasks, goals, and decisions: climbing the ladder.
7. Complacency: Beware of "good enough."
8. The joy factor: Vitamin D for the soul.
9. Great success is never easy. Easy success is less enduring.
10. Principles: Your word must have weight for your actions to possess nobility.
11. You did it! Now what? The role of legacy.

●●●

In America, the road to stardom feels innate. Every athlete, particularly an inner-city youth, knows the drill; it has taken on a mythology all of its own.

That myth didn't exist in Britain. Athletic kids dream of being the next Tim Henman (only better at Wimbledon) or, these days, famous footballers for Manchester United, Liverpool, or Chelsea.

I didn't have the faintest notion of how to actually get to the NBA. All I knew was that it was the pinnacle of what had suddenly become my chosen profession, far above any European league. All of which forced me to be more diligent than American kids.

In the American dream, anyone can become president, Donald Trump, or Michael Jordan. All it takes is hard work and a little talent. Hoop dreams require dominance in high school and college, plus a lot of practice, weight lifting, and perfecting acrobatic dunks and three-point shots. Then, boom, you're there.

If only it were so straightforward. The real process, I soon discovered, is much more complicated. In addition to talent and hard work, it's about having the right support system, foresight, and plain old dumb luck.

The ones who get caught up in the myth are the ones who are going to fail to do what it takes. They are the young players who believe that Globetrotter-style ball will get them to the top. It does get them to the top—the top of playground fame, but not the NBA.

Superstars can afford to believe their own myth. It's precisely that kind of arrogance that makes them unstoppable. They have the one-in-a-million talent to make it happen, sometimes even regardless of their discipline—or lack of it. But for most of the more ordinary athletes, the key is to eliminate the myth from the pursuit. You actually have to stop seeing the NBA for its bling: adoration, endless sex with gorgeous women, flashbulb dunks, VIP lists at clubs, the black Escalades.

While those things exist, they are a tiny slice of NBA life. The reality is much less glamorous. It's about never being out of shape, monitoring every calorie, working around the clock, endless jet lag, playing with pain, ruthless competition, lack of privacy, daily scrutiny, grinding pressure. If that's not enough, there are the family sacrifices, the difficulties in distinguishing friends from fakes.

The real benefits are the ones you don't hear much about because they are not part of the fantasy. They are much more subtle than fans would ever imagine or care to imagine. If you make the most of them, they can actually be the platform for you to communicate ideas and principles to young people, to display, through your play and your community work, what it means to be a responsible adult with the resources to make a difference.

Also, the financial security enables you to make a difference in your own creative way—one of the most rare privileges life presents.

At its worst, the dream is a cruel hoax. If you really want to screw a bunch of poor black kids, tell them to focus on basketball when only one in a thousand will even make it to the college level, let alone secure a scholarship. It's a great way to make sure there'll be plenty of street cleaners and burger flippers. There's nothing wrong with that kind of honest work, except the low income and lack of benefits. But when dead-end jobs become destiny, that's when hope departs and despair takes root.

Part of the myth is that the only thing that matters is basketball; education is simply a distraction, an obligation that must be fulfilled to meet the minimum graduation requirements.

The truth is that life begins *after* basketball. The average career of an NBA player is only a few years, and the NBA is littered with guys who show up for a week, a training camp, a 10-day contract, never to be heard from again.

I always laughed when people asked about my "backup" plan, given that any fallback would represent the vast majority of my life, even if I were fortunate enough to play into my 30s.

CHAPTER 6 ●●● ⌉ Coming to
⌋ America

To me, America amounted to David Hasselhoff and the A-Team.
Based on Hasselhoff's television series Knight Rider, I thought
souped-up Pontiacs were America's version of the Rolls Royce.

In *The Guardian*, I read that the president of the United States
was an actor and a friend of Margaret Thatcher. I knew there were
a lot of people called "vets" running around, because America
fought lots of wars.

It didn't take long to have some of my stereotypes confirmed
and others obliterated. Shortly before I was due to graduate
from Stockport in 1988, at the age of 17, I landed in Chicago,
where, circling the airport, I found a procession of shiny white

limos—still rare back home. I was shocked at what seemed like the wealth of all Americans. It would be several years before I saw the other side of the tracks.

I caught a small commuter plane to a basketball camp at Roanoke College in Virginia. There I hoped to expand my skills while checking out a high school that had offered me a spot.

It was mid-summer. Within five minutes of getting out of the car, I was drenched in sweat. The humid air was thicker than Mum's beef stew.

A local family had agreed to put me up at their home. It was dark when I arrived a few miles outside of Roanoke. And after a home-cooked meal, I went straight to bed, exhausted, without looking around much.

When I woke up, I could barely believe my eyes. In the light of day, I found myself in the biggest house I'd ever seen outside Buckingham Palace. I couldn't believe *one* family had so much space.

The house stood on what must have been a hundred acres. There were pastures leading to rolling hills leading to more pastures. Cows grazed contentedly. Horses dotted the landscape, and this was right outside a bustling city.

When I sat in the car of their son, Robbie, a fellow ballplayer, it took awhile to get over the fact that this 16-year-old had a car of his own. Back home, Mum, well off by most standards, drove a beat-up car. Few kids in England ever got their own auto, and all I could think about was the time wasted getting rides and waiting for buses all over Manchester.

In America, it seemed, everyone had a car, regardless of race, economic status, or age. And not just any car. They were all luxury cars or sports cars or jeeps.

I was almost strangled by a seat belt that closed over my shoulder. Gears shifted automatically. What's more, the car had a built-in machine that cooled the air. It was my first brush with air conditioning, which would become my constant companion as I toured the nation's hottest climates.

Everything was super-sized. It was the land of vast expanses of open space, big cars, huge houses, and oversized sports arenas. The gym at Roanoke College, featuring a mammoth bubble dome, was the biggest I'd ever stepped inside.

I was convinced *Americans are so rich it's outrageous.* I didn't know whether to be impressed or appalled, so I adopted a measure of both, an attitude about the paradoxical nation I would carry with me for years.

Even more foreign to me was the Southern accent. For the first week I could barely understand a word anyone said, figuring out my cues more by context and body language. I smiled and nodded my way through conversations.

Even the food was strange. I was shocked to find blueberries buried in the biggest, spongiest confections I'd ever tasted. These muffins were heaven in tiny round cakes, especially when they were toasted and smeared with butter. I'd never imagined peanut butter and jelly (known as "jam" back home, where "jelly" is Jell-O) could taste so fantastic together, especially when surrounded by thin layers of Wonder Bread. It was the start of another chapter in my love affair with carbs.

I got a warm welcome on and off court. Even though I was hardly the best player, once again there was a sense that I was a jewel in the rough, a guy who could be made into a star with proper coaching and enough practice. I received the camp's Most Improved award, although that was probably as much of a function of the impression left by college recruiters who shadowed my every move as it was of my play.

My limitations were also very much on display: I was foolish enough to enter the dunk contest—not a good idea for a black guy who jumps like a white guy. Although by then I could dunk easily, backward and forward, it was no surprise when I did not win. The acrobatic dunks fans have come to expect were beyond me.

After more than a year of shuffling around archaic facilities, I was shocked to find out that we could play all day and all night. After roll call at 7:15 a.m., we hit the courts, virtually all day long. Replete with gleaming hardwood floors and glass backboards, the courts were perfectly maintained and lighted.

When camp ended, the hard sell began. The local private high school wanted me to sign, and the coach treated me to a gourmet lunch, jet skiing, and sailing on a huge reservoir.

Better still, Robbie was, well, as hot as the climate, but since I still had little notion of sexuality, alas that notion did not dawn on me until I'd left Roanoke.

This truly was the land of milk and honey.

At the end of my two-week stay, I boarded a twin-engine plane for Toledo, Ohio, via Columbus. The plane was the only scary thing about the entire trip. It rattled and rocked the whole way, and I gripped the seat until my knuckles ached.

The head coaches at St. John's Jesuit and St. Francis, two Catholic high schools, met me at the tiny airport. I was greeted in what seemed to be yet another foreign tongue in the same country. *Did every state have a different accent?* I'd finally mastered Virginia-speak, only to find myself stymied by an even thicker Midwestern accent.

I spent time with the St. Francis coach first, chatting at his bachelor pad. He made me feel at home by offering me tea, until what he actually served turned out to be tall glass filled with a sickly sweet brown concoction over ice.

They call this tea? Blasphemy!

I muttered *my God* to myself at the sight of a copy of *Playboy* sitting on the coffee table, as though it was just another piece of reading material.

He smiled and ticked off the virtues of St. Francis, which included several city championships, first-class academics, and a history of getting players to the "next level." It was a pitch I would hear in many variations over my career from coaches and recruiters, but it never once sounded convincing. Why do recruiters always think a fantasy is more convincing that reality?

During this leg of the tour, I stayed with the wonderful family of a kid on the St. Francis team, Jerome. There were many more offerings of glasses of sticky iced tea.

As we ate barbequed chicken in the backyard, the most aggressive mosquitoes I'd ever come across feasted on what must have seemed like a bonanza of flesh.

On Sunday morning, Jerome's mom invited me to join them at one of the churches that dotted the landscape. Protesting that I didn't have my Sunday best, I told them they should go without me. When they returned, overdressed for God, she spotted my suit, buried underneath some T-shirts in my luggage. She seemed hurt and confused.

I was afraid to tell her the truth. My image of American religion was faith healing, fainting, and speaking in tongues. Raised in a secular home dominated by the scientific ethic, I wanted no part of such nonsense.

When I eventually did get around to attending a black Baptist church, my stereotypes were debunked. I was moved by the music, by the sense of common purpose, and the eloquent exhortations of charity. I grew to love visiting churches, temples, and synagogues for the architecture and the pageantry alone. The solidity and serenity of the buildings and the services is often astounding. But following Mum's lead, I was far too much of a skeptic to become a true believer. Focused as I was on a decidedly material goal, I was hardly going to rest my future on faith in a higher power that, even in the unlikely case it existed, was even more unlikely to take interest in the ups and downs of a young man whose primary goal in life was putting a large leather ball through a small metal hoop.

As my career progressed and an athletic form of muscular Christianity reared its dubious head in the pro locker room, I could only shake my head. Here we were, engaged in a pursuit that to an unparalleled degree was based on our own hard-earned human abilities, yet they were attributing their play to a dubious otherworldly entity. And, given our paychecks, none of us were about to fit through the eye of a needle.

I preferred to find my spirituality in music. Jerome took me along to visit a friend who had an electronic beat box set up in his van. They launched into a rap, the first I'd ever heard. It was a glorious display of spontaneous poetry, something beyond my meticulous mind. I listened in awe, wondering whether I could ever do something that cool. I didn't want to end up what I was that day—the guy who just sits, listens, and taps his feet.

It dawned on me how different yet similar two people can be. We both had African roots (mine were somewhat closer to "the motherland" than theirs, but who's counting?). Yet that musical tradition wasn't part of the culture in which I'd been raised. I didn't know rap from Republicans. I was more likely to break into a chorus of *Seven Brides* than Ice Cube.

Beyond all that, though, Jerome and I had much in common, from basketball to an appreciation of our growing friendship. We had such a blast together that I was sorry I didn't join him at St. Francis.

In the end I had opted for St. John's. The head coach, Ed Heintschel, was a Joe Forber-like figure. When he promised to help me become the player and the person I wanted to be, as long as I put in the effort, I could feel his sincerity.

What cinched the deal is that he was the antithesis of the hard sell. He made no promises or assurances of a college scholarship and NBA fame and fortune, making clear that I'd chosen a treacherous path but that he'd be there to help me every step of the way.

CHAPTER 7 ●●●| The Smooch

After I enrolled at St. John's, I moved in with the Releford family in Swanton, Ohio, 35 minutes by car from school. The house was surrounded by several acres. A basketball court looked over a man-made lake.

I couldn't believe my good fortune when Mrs. Releford led me to my own spacious room, complete with a mini black-and-white television.

Luke Releford was team captain and star forward. When I'd been on my recruiting trip a few months earlier, Luke had led me to believe that we liked the same music, sacrificing his taste to make me feel welcome. Now that he had his center under his roof, all he wanted to play was hard rock. He wasn't at all keen on listening to one of my favorites, Michael Jackson's *Thriller*, as he drove me to school every morning in his old purple Z roadster.

I was addicted to '80s pop, especially the Brit variety, which at that time had barely made it to the American coasts, let alone the middle of the county. So I suffered from serious music withdrawal. In those pre-iPod days, I missed the cool tunes of Ultra Vox, Hot Chocolate, Marc Almond, Human League, Erasure, and ABBA.

In retrospect, I suppose my taste in music should have been an early clue. It was hard to imagine a gayer playlist than the one I'd unconsciously assembled.

●●•

During lunch period one day, a teammate directed me to what was euphemistically known as the "black table," even though my friends from the team were scattered across the cafeteria. I had friends who sat at that table, but skin color seemed a poor excuse for social groupings. After all, I'd come to America to try my hand at one of the most multicultural professions in the world, one that would become even more diverse in the near future.

I resented and resisted being categorized. As a brown kid raised by a white mother, being defined by the color of one's skin made no more sense than being defined by my size. I had come to America, the land of the free, to create my own identity, and now I was being pushed into a box.

I learned some harsh lessons at that table as we chowed down on overcooked vegetables, hamburgers, and another uniquely American creation, decadent and brilliant: chocolate and milk. The police, I was soon informed, didn't much like black people. If they pulled you over, you must be sure to place your hands out the window so they can be seen. "Don't give them any excuse to open fire," one kid put it bluntly.

It was at that table that I learned that to be black meant I was somehow less of a human being, except when it came to criminality, when we were most assuredly more.

Back in England, the social pressure was different. In secondary school, a boy once wrote the word "nigger" on a sticker and stuck it on my back. I was mad, and nearly as soon as I reported him, he was suspended. But the general feeling was: *How pathetic. How sad for him.*

More than a decade later, he sent me a letter apologizing profusely for what he'd done, and I readily accepted it. The guy had punished himself enough, and I appreciated the sentiment.

Needless to say, I didn't need to be told gay was worse even than brown, black, or yellow. "Homo" and "queer" were universal put-downs. Like my pop music, AIDS was a distant echo from the coasts of America that seemed to give those epithets unspoken force.

I learned the hard way about the word "fag." A bunch of kids were smoking cigarettes during break behind the school. "They're smoking fags," I said, casually, to a classmate. Back home, "fag" is slang for cigarette. He shot back a frown supplemented by a cross-eyed look.

The confusion was funny because it pointed out how arbitrary the meaning of any word really is. But it was also sad, another instance of categorizing others negatively for no relevant purpose other than to cover someone's own insecurity. In high school culture, differences for which moral connotations were drawn abounded: goths, geeks, nerds, athletes, drama types.

The anti-gay animus made me realize that there was yet another way in which I might somehow be different from the rest. But, unlike my size, which was only too obvious, at that point any glint of recognition was purely internal. Externally, I was the last person to evoke suspicion. Athletes were considered the top of the teenaged food chain, and my British-ness made me especially hard to categorize.

It was also pretty hard to bully this enormous, wide-shouldered man-child, no matter how gentle I came across. And since I'd put my "whale" era behind me, I was generally accorded a great deal of respect—deference even. There were straight guys with less bulk, some of whom conformed to gay stereotypes, who were hassled. Meanwhile, the oversized gay kid got away scot-free.

My status as an athlete made it surreal to know that if others knew this inconsequential truth about me, I would suddenly drop to the bottom of the heap, as though the gender of the person I fancied had anything to do with my character and accomplishments.

It was probably a good thing, then, that I didn't fully grasp my own reality. My lack of self-knowledge was a blessing in disguise. It allowed me to block out negative perceptions of myself and stay focused on the reason I was there: to earn a college scholarship. Perhaps if I'd had a fuller understanding, like many high school kids today, I would have steered clear of organized sports entirely, knowing that a happy, fulfilling future lay elsewhere.

Even for all the hostility in the world of a Catholic boys' school, hints of homosexuality were never far. One day I wandered into the locker room after spending a Saturday morning practicing my free throws. I was not the only one who thought I had the gym to myself. As I pushed open the swinging doors, two guys from the wrestling team were locked in a passionate kiss. The door swung shut and I backed out, pretending not to see. But I was sure: *Two guys were smooching!* I'm not talking an innocent peck on the cheek. I'm talking an innocent moment of pure lust.

Those guys are pretty pent up, I thought to myself. In reality, I might have been talking about myself. It was electrifying, I had to admit, but it didn't seem to apply to me. I figured it must a wrestling thing.

Early that year I had actually attended a wrestling match. I sat in the stands imagining my own heroics on the floor where they'd set up the mat. (Basketball season opened in a few weeks.) Then I noticed that one of the wrestlers had an erection. Not that I was looking. The shape of their skin-tight singlets made it impossible to ignore.

I looked right. I looked left. Everyone seemed oblivious to the, uh, elephant in the room. A college wrestling friend later told me that it was an unavoidable part of a sport in which young men engage in an intensely physical, and extremely close, activity. But at the time it simply seemed bizarre.

Brit kids are especially aware of the reputation of boys' schools. But wrestlers aside, it was a chaste time for me and, I suspect, most of my classmates.

I was there for a reason. I knew that if I got fat, out of shape, or distracted, I was going home. The only thing that would keep me in America and on my NBA track was my dedication to The Plan and to the program coach had laid out for me.

I didn't allow myself to feel much that year. There were no schoolboy crushes. Even if I had had one, I would hardly have expected reciprocity. And in some ways, even though I was excelling on court—and the baby fat was falling away like excess baggage—I still saw myself as a freak. I wasn't the kind of guy people fancied.

In biology class, I sat next to Aaron, who drew cute cartoon faces on my books, and I was charmed. It was all so sweet. We became pals, but that's as far as it went. I can't even say I imagined him naked.

The opposite sex was no more on my mind. Knowing I was only going to be there that year, I kept mostly to myself. Which was easy because there was not exactly a lot of teenaged girls hanging around a boys' school.

●••

Put simply: I had one six-month season to prove I belonged at a college powerhouse.

Every moment I wasn't studying or sleeping was dedicated to basketball practice. During class breaks we'd play pick-up in the gym. By the time I was back in a classroom, my clothing would be soaked through to the skin.

I had a long way to go. I loved to float on the perimeter, looking for my shot, surprisingly deft and accurate, especially for a big man with a reconstructed shooting hand.

That was the reverse of what was expected of big men, at least in that era. Today it's not unusual to find seven-footers like Dirk Nowitzki knocking down threes. Ed was encouraging, believing I'd accomplished the hard part first. Learning to bang down low would be easier, and more about strength, timing, footwork, and aggressiveness than the God-given touch of shooting.

The American game was so fast that it bordered on frantic. At the same time, it was more physical and more athletic—basically, better in every way, primarily because of superior facilities, coaching, and a far larger pool of talent from which to draw. As I saw it, basketball had eclipsed baseball and football among many young people as the coolest sport.

In early games I was taking only half a dozen or so shots, averaging close to six points. The team already had a starting center, Jamie Happ, and Ed worked me into the rotation. I was acutely aware of Jamie's feelings. The writing was on the wall; he'd lost his coveted starting role before the regular season had even started. It was his senior year, and at that age varsity status is a badge of honor. It would have been natural to resent the touted outsider, who had at least half a foot on him, brought in to upgrade *his* position.

Yet he was the first person to familiarize me with the offense, fine-tune a move, offer a kind word. I was astonished at how gracefully he handled the demotion. I wondered: Were the tables turned, would I have been as big a man?

In December we took a bus to Florida for the Kingdom of the Sun Tournament. As we drove across the icy highways of the Midwest, I wondered how anyone could use "sun" to describe a winter tournament—until we crossed the Florida state line.

It wasn't just *any* sun. There was more natural light than I had ever imagined, eclipsing the height of the British summer. Everything was illuminated; shadows were overpowered. I was so freaked out that I took shelter in my room, where I lounged on the bed and watched the huge color TV while everyone else was downstairs in the pool.

At that time, Paula Abdul's "Opposites Attract" video seemed to stream endlessly on MTV. In a fit of optimism, the lyric "We come together/Cuz opposites attract" seemed to sum up my relationship with my newly adopted country.

I'd been enjoying the Toledo winter wonderland. The snow and ice made for treacherous driving, but for me it meant school-free storm days and Christmas for months longer than in Manchester. Now we'd gone from snowstorm to sauna.

Sensing my discomfort, Ed came up to my room to make sure I was okay. I wasn't about to explain my pool phobia, so I took a deep breath and went out wrapped in a towel. It was too damn hot to stay covered for long. I jumped in the pool, where everyone splashed deliriously, hollering "Marco Polo." I didn't understand anything about the game except there was lots of yelling. But I enjoyed it enough to temporarily lose my self-consciousness.

Suitably relaxed, we were ready to go when game time rolled around the next day. We squared off against a very good team from the District of Columbia with an equally good center, Michael Smith, who ended up in the NBA.

I played him to a standoff. I was hitting my jumper, but I also made a point of going man-to-man down low, rebounding and defending with abandon. It was a huge confidence booster, and we took down a touted foe.

Playing more freely and aggressively than ever before, I hadn't dominated to such an extent since Fog Lane Park. To be fair, there were only a few solid big men in the Toledo city league. NBA standouts such as Jimmy Jackson had come out of our league the year before, but at the time I was one of the few.

My play was starting to draw attention. Scouts lined the court during practice and games. It wasn't long before boxes of material from many of the country's college programs were arriving at St. John's.

After starring in front of 2,000 at a University of Toledo tourney, I received a letter signed by none other than Bobby Knight himself. Even I knew he was a big deal, and that he only recruited the very best. Yet I also knew he was not the kind of coach I could tolerate, even if there was no disputing that he knew how to win. I'd heard about his abusive antics, recalling Mr. Shackelford and all my boyhood tormenters.

Joe and Ed showed me there was a more humane, respectful way to get to the same place. Winning really was everything, but only if it was accomplished honorably.

I would have my choice of coaching styles. The Plan was working to perfection. The recruitment process had begun.

●●•

Things were not as smooth at the Relefords. By January, Mrs. Releford left my meals in the kitchen while the rest of the family ate around the dinning room table. I would dine alone in my bedroom in front of the little TV. Luke and I had stopped talking, and the rest of the family rallied around him.

There was an unacknowledged sense that as the new leader of the team getting the most attention, I had somehow stolen Luke's thunder. It was not exactly a Jamie Happ moment. But I didn't blame Luke at all.

His parents believed I had ruined their son's chances of getting a scholarship to Indiana, but in truth, Luke was no Damon Bailey.

Then again, neither was I. But I was six-foot-ten; Luke was half a foot shorter.

I felt a creeping sense of loneliness in that house—with a measure of homesickness thrown in. So it was with glee that I looked forward to Mum's visit in late January. She came bearing English-style gifts for the Relefords—lace from London, pottery from Hornsey. They went over well, but the atmosphere, even with Mum around, remained frosty.

I skipped school and we spent entire days at the local Bob Evans, where I ascended to pancake heaven. Since the tea was terrible, we drank coffee from morning until late afternoon, chatting the day away. It was as if sunshine poured down on me in the middle of winter.

I told her about Florida and Bobby Knight and the potential college suitors. I showed her clippings from the local newspapers about my exploits.

She beamed. Less than two years earlier I'd never touched a basketball and my heart had been set on becoming a child psychologist. It was a bit of a stretch, even for my doting mother, to imagine her awkward, uncoordinated kid playing big-time ball.

But her faith was unshakeable, and that made me feel invincible.

Not long after Mum left, I began spending more time at the home of Ed and his wife, Cheryl, and their children. The highlight of my Midwestern experience was going to a pristine lake in neighboring Michigan, where Ed's mum, Nana, owned a house. She made the most amazing homemade buns with white frosting. After devouring several along with coffee, Ed took me turtle hunting. We roamed the edges of the lake in a canoe, heading up tributaries searching for the shy creatures. Then we scooped them up in a net, placing them on the bottom of the canoe. They had no way of knowing whether soup was on the menu, so I couldn't blame them for snapping at our toes.

Since I didn't like killing them for sport or for soup, we took them home for boasting photos and then released them back into the lake.

I sometimes wondered if this is what it felt like to have a dad. For all those kids out there with dads, I hoped so.

Soon I moved in with Randy Felhaber, the son of our assistant coach, Bud Felhaber, and Randy's wife, Judy. The couple did not have kids yet, so they lavished attention on me, becoming a kind of surrogate family. I felt like a spoiled only child. I went through all the adolescent stages—playing hoops with Randy, helping Judy out in the kitchen, and begging to be allowed to drive the family car.

In my nine months in America's heartland, I had the best teenage experience I could imagine, earned the attention of big-time colleges, and was surrounded by some of the best people anyone could hope to meet. I may not have been as religious as my uniformly Christian hosts, but I was blessed anyway.

One day, on a bus ride to a game, one of my teammates, Jack Johnson, fell asleep, his head coming to rest on my shoulder. Awakened by a bump, he looked at me as if to ask whether it was okay. I nodded, and he fell back asleep. I thought little of that moment until several months later. Jack, a sophomore, was hanging out on a street corner playing cards with a bunch of older guys. Gunfire erupted from a passing car. Although he was not the target, Jack's body was in the way of the speeding bullet. He died instantly at the age of 15.

Thus began my love affair with the National Rifle Association.

I had already realized that America was a land of extremes. Whether it was cars or hoops, Americans went all out. It was generally a trait I admired—and emulated. Who would not want to excel on the biggest and greatest stage the world had ever seen?

But there was also a downside. Jack's death highlighted a violent and gun-obsessed subculture, and the politics that not only permitted but glorified it. It seemed everyone I met had been touched by gun violence.

As I stood at the funeral and watched this young man laid to rest, I realized this was another mythic American story. How many similar victims were buried every day?

The notion that guns increased safety was as absurd as the notion that every inner city black kid has a legitimate shot at the NBA. Guns aren't shields. They don't prevent violence. They exacerbate it.

The next year, after St. John's, I worked on a Tennessee farm during the summer (yes, another scalding climate) to earn some spending money. The owner of the property took me along on a trip to "take care" of some rattlesnakes, by which he meant shooting them with his handgun.

He offered to give me a lesson, so I took aim at a tin can set up on a log. My first shot missed its mark. The second hit the can dead on, and it exploded into the air. It was intoxicating and terrifying at the same time. I felt like a superhero—precisely the problem with weapons. I was as afraid of learning to enjoy that feeling as I was of the gun itself.

I laid down the weapon and walked away. I vowed that only time I would see one again would be in the movies.

Jack's death marred an otherwise brilliant season, and we dedicated every game to his memory. I dominated down low while Shane Komives, the son of the great Butch Komives, lit it up from the perimeter. It was a tough combination for teams to guard, and we beat up on pretty much everyone.

In the finals we were matched up against archrival Scott at their home court. It was a seesaw battle down to the final seconds. Scott got the ball at half court, down by one. The ball went to John White, a name now seared into my memory, who threw up a Hail Mary shot that somehow swished through the hoop.

The buzzer sounded. The fans went nuts, pouring onto the court in celebration.

In the locker room after the game, I didn't bother to hide the tears that flowed down my face. Accustomed to carrying the team on my shoulders, I'd played my heart out. I couldn't escape the feeling that I'd let everyone down.

We'd played well, nothing to be ashamed of. But I felt exhausted, demoralized, and angry. We deserved a fairy tale ending. I deserved a fairy tale ending. Surely life rewarded the deserving?

Apparently not.

CHAPTER 8 ●●●] Varsity Blues

In early 1989, I took recruiting calls on speakerphone in Ed's office so he could monitor their propriety. The pitches were all pretty similar. I listened as the flattery poured forth.

"We've been monitoring your progress and we like what we see."

"Your style is the perfect match for us."

"You're quite a ballplayer."

"We can make you into something special."

They were each reading from more or less the same script and drawing from similar scouting reports in hope of filling their scholarship quotas.

I had shady visits from smaller schools, usually late at night in the corner booths of chain restaurants. School "representatives" would talk, euphemistically of course, about the potential financial benefits of playing for schools with "generous alums." I'm not sure why I didn't storm out of the place, because when you've glimpsed your soul in the dark, it shouldn't be for sale at any price.

What mattered was finding the right match. I had my heart set on Wake Forest. With its sprawling campus, first-rate athletic program, and distinguished psychology department, it seemed a perfect fit. However, Wake Forest only recruited really good basketball players, not just really tall ones. I flirted briefly with going West, where I would have loved to attend UCLA. But that school only recruited high school All-Americas, something I'd lacked the talent to achieve.

Yet there was no shortage of suitors. Duke, Indiana, and Penn State all came calling. At James Madison, Lefty Driesell promised me the moon, but I had my feet firmly planted on earth. Boston College made inquiries, and there was a romantic side of me that made going home appealing, even if I had little recollection of my city of birth.

Somewhere along the way, I had a particularly good visit with Eddie Fogler of Vanderbilt. He was billed as a disciple of Dean Smith, the visionary North Carolina coach. How could you go wrong with that?

The university dovetailed neatly with my criteria from The Plan. It had a solid psychology department and a strong Division I basketball program in the Southeastern Conference, where I could develop against the best young centers in the nation, including a young Shaq. Vanderbilt seemed quite promising.

●●●

Thank goodness basketball is played indoors. Nashville had to be the hottest of all the hot spots I'd been.

Mum was less than thrilled about my being in the buckle of the Bible belt. Perhaps thinking back to the racial polarization of her Boston days, she worried about a brown man living in the South, concerned that I wouldn't be given a fair shake or might even end up the victim of racial violence.

Perhaps she was unaware that black athletes—if not black Americans—are treated like royalty, especially in the South. There is still plenty of racism, but the days of official segregation ended after Oscar Robertson and Wilt Chamberlain could play in a city but not eat at its restaurants.

The Harlem Globetrotters, once composed of blacks banned by pro leagues, were still going strong, but not by necessity.

Blacks had gone from being viewed as intellectually inferior to athletically superior (*and* intellectually inferior)—nearly as dubious a proposition.

When it came to race, Nashville was indeed more than a little tense. The white college kids were often from rich families, drove expensive cars, and ate at nice restaurants even though they didn't work. Blacks were concentrated in blue-collar jobs and spent a lot of time serving the students. There were minority students, but they were outnumbered by a sizeable margin.

I myself got a pass. Because I'm so obviously British in accent and manner, white Americans lacked the stereotypes to view me as somehow menacing. I'd been written up in the college paper, and they knew I was a little eccentric. I read books, drank tea, and wrote poetry—not the sort of activities attributed to marauding black youth.

The double standard would have been funny were it not so sad. I'd watch white people cross the street when I approached—only to cross back to avoid other black folks.

At the same time, there was something special about the city, which has a languid atmosphere and plenty of cultural attractions. I took to Southern cuisine, which seemed exotic compared to the PB&J and chocolate milk of the Midwest. Homemade cornbread slathered with butter is the South's blueberry muffin—sweet and savory.

Walking around the sprawling Vanderbilt campus, I found the people to be warm and open, and if their reaction to my presence was any indication, they adored their college athletes.

●●●

Who makes a big man look good on court? The coach? Fans? It's up to you to play well. But the wizard who controls the ball, the point guard, also has a major say by getting you the rock—or failing to get it to you—when you're in position to score.

The moment I met Matt Maloney, the summer before my first Vanderbilt fall semester, I knew I'd found my roomie. He was a heavily recruited point guard from New Jersey. The fact that his father was an assistant coach at Temple made him even more appealing.

Our room was a box with two single beds and one window overlooking the lush campus. A well-used phone hung on the wall. My side of the room was adorned with a massive poster of a blue whale, the planet's largest mammal and my personal mascot. It was surrounded by *Sports Illustrated*'s latest stories about the great Karl Malone, The Mailman, and Randy White, a player doomed by the name Mailman II. I had no intention of becoming Mailman III.

The arrangement would have been bliss, if only I could understand what the hell Matt was talking about in his thick New Jersey accent. I was proud of mastering the Southern and Midwestern accents, and now I was confronted by another mysterious dialect. And Americans think *we're* the ones with accents!

As I struggled to decipher Matt, Mr. Maloney smiled in amusement. "Don't worry, son, you will learn," he promised. "You are family now."

He was true to his word. The Maloneys took care of me. They were the very definition what Mum called "good people."

While the motive behind my choice of roommates might have been pragmatic, Matt and I quickly became genuine pals. I admired his forthrightness. If you failed to respect him, he would let you know in the form a fist to the face. You knew where his loyalty lay because he always had your back.

We passed the time talking ball, plotting world domination, and just hanging out over coffee. (I'd given up trying to get real tea down South.) There was no limit to his athletic ambition, no pretense that he was here just to have fun, although he was hardly averse to it.

And there was plenty to be had. Matt was far more outgoing than I, and just days into the semester he was already dragging me along to hang with his ever-widening circle of friends. He dated the first real Southern belle I'd ever met. I got a kick out of seeing them together: the well-mannered blond girl, a cheerleader no less, alongside the fast-talking Jersey dude, the personification of culture clash.

That didn't leave a lot of time for me, especially because, still a recluse at heart, I turned down many invitations to join his crowd for nights out. After awhile, he started asking less often, and I sulked until I confronted him and we had it out. I remained upset until a mutual friend wisely suggested I meet Matt half way. If I accepted more of his invitations, he'd hang out with me more often.

I learned a lot about friendship that year. In some ways, Matt reminded me of Peter in his ability to bring me out of my shell. He challenged my tendency toward isolation and introspection without invading my cherished sense of privacy.

I even found a girlfriend, a member of the woman's basketball team named Justine. She was tall, graceful, and beautiful. When she moved, on and off the court, it was as if she floated, and it was no surprise when she became homecoming queen.

And, yes, it was sexual. At the time I desperately sought companionship, and in Justine I found someone I cared about and who wanted to take care of me. Our intimacy was more an expression of that kind of love than a true indication of my sexual orientation, especially because we were both very naïve about all things erotic. She was not some substitute for the real thing—I loved her very much. She was not simply someone I used to cover for my *true* sexuality—something I didn't understand at the time anyway.

Suffice to say, however, my kissing skills had not improved.

●●●

The vertical leap from high school to college was exponential. It was larger than the difference between college and the NBA, at least for me.

Everything was bigger and faster. But it was also a different sport. I had to adjust to the concept of illegal zone defenses, the three-point line, the 24-second-clock, all modeled on the NBA. It didn't help that I'd been relatively sheltered at St. John's. In fact, it wasn't until I reached Vanderbilt in the fall of 1989 that I even knew there was such a thing as March Madness.

Stamina is one of those things you assume you have until proven otherwise. I'd improved my conditioning in Toledo, but was caught off guard by Fogler's brutal two-a-day workouts, before and after lunch, and the additional, endless weight lifting and sprints. At times it felt like more exertion than my still-flabby body could endure. At least one guy would puke at every practice.

I appreciated the hard work. But Fogler made the classic coach's mistake of equating discipline with sadism. He fancied himself a taskmaster in the Dean Smith mould. But he was Dean Smith with a mean streak, while lacking the great man's charisma and vision.

The assistant coach at Vanderbilt, Rich Callahan, was even worse. In his mind, I was too "nice" to be a real ballplayer, a backhanded compliment if I'd ever heard one. In one drill, we leaped into lay-ups while the defender pummelled us. If the defender didn't hit hard enough, he himself would be pummelled, so players were brutal to each other just to avoid Callahan's wrath.

This was like secondary school rugby practice all over again. I never could see the point of these adult versions of "smear the queer." It had nothing at all to do with basketball and everything to do with Callahan's own cruelty.

When it came my turn to hit someone, I made it clear I'd prefer not to. My teammates later reported that Callahan made fun of my British accent after I walked off the court in protest. Sure it was a bit dramatic, but I do have my limits. There's no coach on earth who can make me do something I feel is wrong, and

I soon became convinced that Callahan had no business molding young men.

A negative aura surrounded the team, and it showed on the court. I wasn't helping much, either, playing like the raw, overmatched freshman I was.

Matt was in a similar predicament. In practice, it was clear he was fast and possessed great ball-handling skills. He was one of the physically strongest point guards around, and he could literally manhandle his smaller counterparts.

If only Fogler agreed. Though we were by no means a great team, Matt and I didn't see much playing time outside practice, and were stuck at the end of the bench.

We'd quickly become black sheep. Shunned by the coaches and even by some of our teammates, we could do nothing but sit together at the end of the bench, plotting our revenge.

Matt and I worked on coordinating our play. We'd get up in the morning, eat breakfast while watching news about the first Iraq war, then head to the gym to shoot, dribble, and work on our two-man game.

Classes still mattered, and I even attended a few the first semester. Then we would eat again, catch a nap, and head to practice. We'd do our best to ignore the atmosphere, knowing we'd have to morph into Isiah Thomas and Larry Bird to have our numbers called.

Then we would head back to the student gym and play pick-up, always on the same team, always releasing our pent-up frustration on anyone foolish enough to rise to the challenge. We knew where we really belonged, and it wasn't in a 7 p.m. pick-up game.

Near the end of the first semester, Fogler called Matt and me into his office. We assumed he was going to tell us we needed to improve our attitude or something along those lines. We had proven beyond a doubt, in practice alone, that we belonged.

"Look, guys, I'm not being cruel," he began.

This was not a good sign.

"I'm trying to be fair. You guys simply are not Division I players. You should be playing Division II or III if you really want to get meaningful playing time."

It was official. We were scapegoats for a disappointing season. In truth, he had no way to accurately evaluate our play with our butts firmly planted on the bench.

Matt protested, but there was no arguing. Coach thought we sucked. Or at least he was using that as the pretext he needed to get rid of us. He wasn't cutting us, in which case he'd have to eat our scholarships, just showing us the door.

In retrospect, the decision just didn't add up. A Dean Smith acolyte ended up telling his only two players who eventually went on to the NBA that they couldn't cut it. (I have to admit to taking guilty pleasure years later when Fogler ended up as a Utah Jazz regional scout just when the franchise signed me to a long-term contract.)

I at least give Fogler credit for telling us what he honestly believed. Far better to let us know we were not part of his plans early enough so we could go somewhere else.

It was a liberating moment. Then and there, we knew our Vanderbilt days most likely were over, and we spent the rest of the year on the athletic department's dime playing and improving every second we got the chance. Fogler and Callahan might not have been able to see it, but we were getting better by the day, rounding into the forces we knew we could become.

Along any path, someone like Fogler will insist you can't get there from here. Some tell you for the right reasons. If you're scared of heights, you probably shouldn't become an astronaut.

But some are more interested in popping your bubble. After the fact, they will take credit for your success, claiming their harsh words cleared your path to greatness by motivating you, when in fact they were a speed bump, at best.

In the film *Junction Boys*, a young Bear Bryant unites his entire high school team against him as a bonding strategy. It was a racially diverse group, and this was the only way he knew how to bring them together. The coach of the 1980 U.S. Olympic hockey team, Herb Brooks, used a similar strategy.

But Bryant and Brooks were clever. Many coaches are not. People who deflate dreams are generally doing it for the pleasure—emotional rape is not too dramatic a term for it—the ultimate power trip. It is way of hiding their own failure, their insignificance and fear.

When I came across people who tried to dissuade me, I remembered one of the tenets of The Plan: By definition, only *I* could have my own best interests at heart. The trick was figuring out how to get there. And whose advice would help you get there first.

My decision to leave Vanderbilt could not have been made without the Maloneys. Over dinner with father and son, I posed the question, "Do we leave or stay and fight?"

"Look at where you stand," Mr. Maloney responded. "Do you believe the people who say you are not any good? Or do you have enough belief in yourself to play for a coach who believes in you?"

He was right. Why submit myself to another season of Fogler's misgivings when I could find a much more positive situation with people who were invested in my success?

Not long after our little chat with Fogler, I was looking to transfer. Once again, academics had taken a back seat to the near-professional level demands of college ball. I signed up only for classes that would get me through the semester, rather than ones I really wanted.

But that didn't stop me from experiencing that familiar sinking feeling when I opened my report card to find a 2.75 GPA. I'd gotten passing grades, thanks to late-night cramming sessions. British schools had prepared me well in *meta* learning (the process of knowing how to learn). I could condense six weeks into six hours—though the results were often less than inspiring.

But in the pursuit of my goal, I'd become single-minded. And I risked disappointing those who had invested so much in my success. I vowed to redouble my efforts wherever I ended up— which was looking increasingly like Penn State.

When I visited in the spring, Penn State was the most lush place I'd ever seen. With 40,000 students, it was big enough to be a town. Surrounded by tree-covered mountains, it felt as if we were in the middle of the wilderness, even though we were not that far from Philadelphia.

Sprawling frat houses with strange Greek letters lined the streets. As I looked over the campus map, it was hard to imagine finding my way around the place, yet I was determined to conquer it, one quadrangle at a time.

This time around, I spent a lot more time scrutinizing the head coach, Bruce Parkhill. On my visit, we sat in the Recreation Hall bleachers, looking down over the rows of blue seats and onto the gleaming court below. "I think I can help make you a very good player," he said. "But I can't promise you a certain role or a certain amount of minutes. You'll have to earn them."

Since prospective coaches had been telling me only what they thought I wanted to hear—that I'd start, play 40 minutes, and then get drafted—Bruce came across as the most honest and sincere of the lot. I was sold without having been sold.

Matt initially also settled on Penn State. We'd spent so much time practicing together that we knew each other's moves like the backs of our hands. We'd created our own system of pick and rolls we were sure would be unstoppable. But when we met up at the Rec Center during that visit, Matt reluctantly told me he'd changed his mind, opting for the University of Pennsylvania instead.

In a flash, I'd gone from teammate to opponent. I fought back tears.

"But you are *my* point guard, you are *my* friend," I sputtered before running off so he wouldn't see me cry.

It wasn't just the way we played ball together. I'd come to enjoy all the familiar stuff of living together: His complaints about my snoring, our caffeine-infused, carbo-loading trips to the pancake house at 4 a.m.

It hurt. I would miss him. But I eventually realized he had to do what was right for him. And I knew we would trade war stories, especially since we were still in the same state. I was sure it wouldn't be long before Matt would make his mark.

And I, too, was on my way.

CHAPTER 9 ●●●] Big Brother

The race was on.

NCAA rules stipulated that transfers must "red shirt," meaning I could practice but not play for the first season. With my lost Vanderbilt year, I was essentially down to three seasons, barring injury, to prove to scouts that I was NBA material.

I bore down like never before, rarely venturing beyond the triangle of class, gym, and library. I treated every practice like a game. We broke up into three teams: white jerseys were the starters, blue their backups. The rest of us, red shirts, walk-ons, various hopefuls, were quite literally green.

If we were playing Princeton next week, it was the green team's responsibility to watch enough video to get down the Tigers' tendencies. We were to give the white team a run for its money, to keep them sharp for the games by mimicking their opponents. In the process, I became a student of the game in a new way. There's something to gaining a distance from the game that can be very valuable, a perspective you lack in the middle of the action, when you are fighting to survive.

Sometimes we played our role too well, basically kicking our teammates' butts. I'm not sure they always appreciated my intensity, but it became a running joke.

Before long, I was scoring at will, even against the first team. "I torched you lot for 116 today," I'd laugh at the end of an hour-long shooting and rebounding spree. And I wasn't even exaggerating.

Wilt Chamberlain move over!

During games I would sit, cheer on my teammates, and do my best to avoid going crazy with the anticipation of getting back into action. It became clear to me, and to everyone on the team, that I was ready for prime time. I was eager for next season, when Bruce had already made clear I was expected to step in as a leader.

Bruce had a nerdy side, and he was always whipping out a notepad he kept in his jacket pocket to scribble down the X's and O's of some new play he'd dreamed up. He became the latest in a long line of mentors, helping me hone my game and become a more well-rounded person. I worked hard to impress him on the court—and refused to disappoint him off it.

The only thing separating me from college stardom, I naïvely believed, was practice. Our team trainer, Chip Harrison, pushed to bring me up to a Division I conditioning level. When I wasn't practicing, I was doing sprints and lifting weights. I took so many shots, the tips of my fingers developed calluses. Whenever I was out of breath, pained by injury, or just ready to junk the whole thing, I'd repeat to myself: *This is how you get great. This is the price of greatness.*

At the same time, I realized all hoops and no play threatened to make John a dull boy. I'd reached the point of diminishing returns from all that practice and working out. And I needed something to focus on when the team was on the road, when I was left back on campus with little to do but study and shoot around by myself.

For many years—practically since I was a kid myself—I'd dreamed of working with disadvantaged youths. Given my background, it was as if I'd been born for the assignment. My father's abandonment, coupled with a mother loving and strong enough to more than make up for the loss, had given me a keen appreciation of family dynamics and the passion to use it to help kids.

Growing up, I'd felt the sting of ridicule. But I'd also benefited from mentors who generously helped lift me out of adolescent despair and into an adulthood filled with promise.

Studying child psychology was no substitute for the real thing. My status as an athlete would give me credibility with young people, and I felt that with the support I'd enjoyed, making my scholarship possible, it was time I repaid my debt to the community.

Years earlier, Penn State assistant football coach Jerry Sandusky founded The Second Mile, a wonderful group that worked to support young people. Jerry invited athletes to hang out with the kids. I got a kick out of the program, which was first-rate, but I wanted more, something that would enable me to make a qualitative difference in kids' lives over time.

Jerry directed me to the local office of Big Brothers/Big Sisters. The organization's caveat was that you had to make a major commitment. It didn't want kids left hanging by college students who thought it would be cool to be a mentor, only to jump ship when it cut into party time. Students would come in, claiming to "love kids," without any sense of how difficult they can be, how frustrating, and how much hard work is involved. The fact is that not all kids are lovable, especially when they are struggling just to survive.

Back in England, holiday public service ads spouted the slogan: "Dogs are for life, not Christmas." If it's true for dogs, it is doubly true for kids.

After the customary four interviews, I was accepted into the program. "Give me the toughest kid you've got," I declared. "I don't want a jelly-and-ice-cream kid."

●••

State College is a typical university town, only bigger. It's home to wealthy business owners, high-salaried tenured professors, and a lot of middle-class university support workers.

I soon learned that, like much of America, there's a seemingly permanent underclass—working people who had moved from Harrisburg, Philadelphia, and Pittsburgh for a chance at a more congenial life in a college town. They were escaping inner cities wracked by poverty, violence, and drugs.

As the area grew, it developed some of the same social dysfunctions. Although people tended to see truant teenagers as the problem, it all started with parents. No matter how many times I visited the homes of those I mentored, their parents were always absent. Sometimes they were working (I could sympathize with that hardship, given my own Mum's long hours). But often they had little interest in raising their children. They behaved as if their kids were not their responsibility, as though they had simply been left on their doorstep in a basket.

I'll never forget the time I spent an evening searching the malls for one 14-year-old. When I finally ran into his mother, she was dressed for a night on the town. When I asked her if she knew where her son was, she looked at me, lip curled, and spat, "Isn't it time for *me* to have a life?" It was not a question.

I soon discovered I had my own flaws, though lack of commitment was not one of them. My first little brother, Joseph, 15, was one of those semi-abandoned kids. He had an exuberant nature and a radiant smile. But he also had a complete inability to focus, even for a few minutes. He refused to let anyone see his feelings, and that built up pressure that resulted in erratic behavior.

He had many of the typical problems associated with troubled adolescents. He smoked pot and drank far too many beers. He skipped school to hang out at the mall. Teachers and kids alike were afraid of him because he had an explosive temper combined with intimidating size and strength.

I spent a lot of time with Joseph and his younger sister, Nancy, trying to provide some structure in their lives. I was there in the morning to make sure he was ready for school. I tried to make sure he was home by a decent hour. I stayed in touch with his mother and teachers.

He seemed to register the fact that I truly cared, which he appreciated. He was particularly pleased that a basketball player cared.

Once in awhile, I'd catch him softening a little, allowing himself to be vulnerable and open to change. But then he would recoil and return to his façade of invincibility.

I blamed myself. Like a struggling substitute teacher, you must establish authority and authenticity right away or you don't stand a chance. He could sense I wasn't quite ready for the task, and he exploited my weakness.

At one point I challenged him on a nasty comment he'd made about another kid. "Rule number one: You just can't say stuff like that," I said.

"Rule number two," he shot back. "Rules don't work."

Joseph was right: Rule number three is that the rules don't always apply.

My comment had come across like I was reading from a book, rather than coming organically from his circumstances. I needed to *show* him why his actions were destructive, not tell him.

I imagine my experience was similar to that of first-time parents—wonderfully happy but woefully unprepared. You can read the books and attend the seminars, but when the bundle is actually there in front of you, it's not so easy. Despite the struggles, I worked with Joseph as long as I could.

I fared better with my next little brother, Anthony, a 14-year-old so charismatic that older teens followed him around, attracted to his sense of danger, risk-taking, and rebelliousness. When I got him not long after Joseph, during my junior year, he was selling drugs to college students (a lucrative market, to be sure) and staying out all night.

I showed up at his house each morning to rouse him for school, and the front door would always be unlocked. Anthony would be passed out on the couch, reeking of booze and cigarettes. I waited as he showered and got ready.

Through Joseph and Anthony, I was introduced to the State College underworld of troubled youth, many of whom became my unofficial little brothers. As the number of my charges grew, one of my professors referred to me as the Pied Piper. I wasn't going to give up on any of them. I was offering no false promises, only all the support one flawed human being could muster.

Over time, my ability to relate and teach improved, and I'd often tour the downtown arcades at night before heading to bed to make sure my kids were not out carousing. I'd round up the stragglers and drive them home, where they belonged. Then I'd be up early the next morning to make sure they got to school.

I became so well known around town that State College police chief Tom King often sought me out. He invited me to join a group of local youth, police, and school leaders who were eager to find new ways of combating truancy and all its associated problems. "You have no idea how helpful you are," he once told me. "My beat cops come in from the street and I ask, 'How's it out there tonight?' And they say, 'Everything's fine. Meech is there.'"

By junior year, I was mentoring six kids in addition to Joseph, who eventually was sent to reform school.

It was a rich life, unfolding along the lines of class, ball, friends, and hanging with my kids. There were times when one area encroached on the others. I'd find myself at the police station dealing with a kid in trouble when I should have been resting, studying, or getting ready for a road trip, or fine-tuning my free throws. Or the opposite: A kid would need help and I'd be unreachable in the middle of Michigan or Ohio.

Fortunately, I'd inherited from my mother the ability to thrive on little sleep, and I could often be found with my light on at 4 a.m., studying, and then up three hours later to drive a kid to school or meet with a teacher.

I felt sorry for "Big" Mike Joseph, my roommate and our backup center. I was difficult, to say the least—strong willed and, frankly, not always pleasant. A bit of a prick, really.

I was forever coming in late, and then my alarm would sound early. My enduring memory of Mike that year was him sitting on his bed with headphones on, probably to drown out my presence.

He was a good man, and we actually got along well. The only time we argued was on the court. He would deny it, but he was a hacker. As the two big men on the team, we had some epic practice battles, and I'd come away with bruises from what were obviously flagrant fouls.

But all the fouls in the world couldn't stop me that year.

"He hacks me because he can't stop me," I'd yell, baiting him to come after me harder.

●●●

The concept of altruism is rubbish. I was helping these kids, to be sure, but I got a massive rush of satisfaction when I made a difference. It was the best feeling in the world—better, I imagined, that winning the Final Four or even an NBA title.

The truth of what Mum had been trying to tell me when I was preparing The Plan emerged: *It was not about me.* When you lose yourself in trying to better the lives of others, it's nothing short of liberating. Suddenly everything makes sense, and the pressure of living up to expectations recedes. Whatever success you might have does not simply feed your own bottomless ego; it can be marshalled on behalf of others.

There were times, though, when I came face to face with my own emotional limits. Human beings have only so much love and compassion. I tried to carefully limit the Big Brother relationships because I knew I would eventually graduate and move on. Any communication we had after that would be sporadic at best.

It was even harder on the other side of the equation. In some cases, this was the younger person's first experience with an adult who cared for them in a responsible, uncomplicated manner. They would begin to show their need just when it was time to disengage. I refused to be the person who was the source of the rejection that sent a kid spiralling, so I made it clear that even though I was moving on, I would never give up on them.

When Mum came to watch me play during my junior year, I was in the throes of detachment anxiety. I asked her how she dealt with her own son moving thousands of miles away.

"My job as a parent is to help my kids fulfil *their* destiny, not *mine*," she said.

She was right. I could stay close to my kids through their accomplishments rather than mere proximity. If I did my job right, I hoped they would go on to lead extraordinary lives.

Before long, word got out about the college basketball star and his gaggle of youth. ESPN sent a camera crew to follow me around as I toured the arcades. A lot of the kids were not mature enough to be on TV, but I allowed the reporter to interview one special young man from New Jersey.

The night of the filming, Joseph's sister sprinted up to me, distraught. Joseph was acting out, so I took off down the street to find him. The camera caught me towering over this little girl and then racing off as I motioned for the crew to stay put.

The emergency turned out to be relatively minor. I found him high and aggressive, pumped up from a fight and angling for another. I was able to settle him down a bit and send him on his way home to sober up.

When I returned to the camera guys, I was breathing heavily and sighing at the pity of lives being wasted. I think the journalists could now see this was not some heart-warming story about a charitable athlete, but instead something much deeper, about desperate young lives at risk.

●••

When I transferred to Penn State, I'd vowed to improve my academic standing as well as my athletic. But the reality of big time college sports is that there is very little time left over for studying.

It seemed we lived on prop planes and buses, moving from state to state, trying to scrunch my frame into tiny seats, catching Z's whenever I could. We'd roll in from another college town at 4 a.m., catch a few more hours of sleep, and then be up in time to make it to class at 8.

When I did find a few hours to crack a book, I was often too exhausted to concentrate. I was forever cramming on buses or planes. I didn't help matters by piling on extracurricular activities and helping to raise half the town.

I wasn't the kind to oversleep. But I would occasionally blow off a class, knowing that on three hours of sleep I would not be productive anyway. I knew when I needed to rest, and I made calculated decisions.

I'd show up during the professor's office hours to explain my absence, and I made sure never to do the athlete's prima donna thing. I was asking kids to be respectful of adults, so I needed to live up to the same standard.

I admit I took a strategic approach to studying, relying on Nittany Notes, State's version of Cliff's Notes, for every major course. When we were snowed in after a night game in Wisconsin, it was really the only way to study for a meteorology class.

Within these confines, I improved dramatically. It helped that I found professors who inspired me. In a rudimentary psychology research methods class, the instructor said, "It's not always the answers that are most important in research, but the question."

This was an insight that would help me in my work with kids. I didn't have answers; they did.

CHAPTER 10 ●●●] # Big Man on Campus

My basketball eligibility coming-out party in 1992 had the Lions matched up at home against highly-ranked Ohio State and its All-America center, Lawrence Funderburke, in a nationally televised game.

I'd already played a few games uneventfully, gained my bearings, but this was the real deal, the start of PSU's inaugural Big Ten season. The Lions lacked a basketball reputation, and Parkhill had set out to change that. This team, built around me, was to start us in that ambitious direction.

I'd spent two inactive years methodically planning for this day. Now I had to make my dreams come true.

Practice had turned upside down. I was the star of the first team now, and I was beating people all over the court. I was dominant enough that Coach Parkhill brought in a sixth defender every time my team ran the offense, so I could prepare for double teams.

On opening night, I began what would become my routine. Pre-game I took a big thermal cup to the sports information office and filled it with coffee. I sat in the lower stands, sipping the liquid, not far from the entrance to our locker room. I watched with awe as the gym filled up and came to life. On my Discman, I sometimes listened to a recording I'd asked the sports psychology department to make, full of inspirational thoughts. But usually I cheated by blasting something more passionate, Sting or the Winans, which never failed to pump me up.

Once the well-wishers became too numerous, I headed to the locker room and sat quietly in front of mine. When we hit the court for warm-ups, it was brilliant to see all these college kids, many from my dorm, lining the court. They were so close that I could reach out and slap them low-fives.

The game against Ohio State found us locked in a seesaw battle. In the closing moments, I surprised everyone by taking two long shots from beyond the three-point arc, nailing both, my unusual long-range shooting touch materializing like lightning in a blue sky.

After the second trey hit net, the capacity crowd erupted. It was so loud that I momentarily wondered whether the roof would come crashing down. We ended up losing, an inexperienced team running out of answers, but we proved we could play with anyone. In all of my fervid imaginings of this moment, I hadn't imagined the intensity of the fans going crazy—especially for me.

Overnight I'd become a celebrity. Around campus, I was already hard to miss because of my height. Now people were stopping me to thank me for those shots. And this after a *loss*. If we put together a winning streak, the house would explode. When I went down with a thud one day in practice, one of my teammates blurted out "OH GOD," as if to underscore my importance to the team.

I loved every second of the adulation, until the downside dawned on me: Now I faced pressure to perform night in and night out.

Against Bobby Knight's Indiana Hoosiers, once again we came up just short, losing in triple overtime. One of our guards dribbled down the sidelines when a defender pulled on his jersey. Swatting the hand away, the ref called a foul on *him*. It was a pivotal play, and we'd been screwed. The replays—printed as stills in the next day's sports pages—clearly showed the jersey grab.

It was a relief to know I didn't always have to shoulder the entire load. Without me on the court, we went on to beat Rashad Griffith in Wisconsin and nationally ranked Minnesota everywhere. Like any young team, we alternately sucked and sparkled.

●●●

Penn State had always been the ultimate football factory, with the great Joe Paterno pumping out a seemingly endless stream of champions.

But by the next season, my junior year of 1994–1995, Big Ten basketball had become the rage. Reeling off a series of victories, we were within spitting distance of a Top 20 ranking. Suddenly the talk on campus was Bobby Knight, the return of the Fab Five, and John Amaechi.

Recreation Hall overflowed with screaming fans. Taking the ball out became an adventure, surrounded by fanatical college students. (I wouldn't have wanted to be an away team. I often overheard them talking about their fear of a sideline ball at Rec Hall.)

It dawned on me that after Paterno, I'd become, arguably, the most recognized face on campus. Football players were bigger stars, to be sure, but other than the quarterback, most were anonymous figures in pads and helmets. I was even bigger than the football players. And 10,000 people saw my face during every home game; exponentially more saw it during televised games.

Such was my celebrity that the college newspaper dreamed up the cute idea making an image of my body into a snow barometer. When we had, say, three feet of snow, the snow would cut just below my waist. Ten feet and I was buried alive!

Being mentioned in the same breath with Paterno was quite a compliment. It was hard not to be impressed with a coaching philosophy that placed academics over athletics, yet still managed to pile up national championships. I even got to know the great coach a little. He'd invite me to make a recruiting call or show up at a football event, and I helped out where I could. I boned up on the game, if only so I could carry on conversations with Paterno and football-obsessed fans. Standing on the sidelines, I tried without luck to figure out its appeal. It reminded me far too much of the brutality of rugby. Compared to basketball, it seemed to lack finesse and grace.

I was relieved to be safely inside Rec Hall on Saturdays because I knew it would be empty, and I could hear the eruptions from fans echoing from the football stadium across the campus as I dribbled and shot alone. It hadn't been all that long ago that I'd been pathetically bribing kids with sweets to be my friends. Now they wanted me to sign their textbooks—and their bodies.

Before I arrived at Penn State, I wondered aloud why stars would often tire of signing autographs when to fans it seemed like a privilege—not to mention an obvious sign that you had made it. Now I understood. Try being asked for the 20th time at 2 in the morning when you are at Gingerbread Man, the local watering hole, trying to enjoy a beer with friends. Endless repetition can take the fun out of even the most special things in life.

Fans are fickle, and they can turn on you as surely as they adore you. In the moment, they believe in you like an evangelical believes in God. But a week or a month later, when you've played poorly or blown a game, you become the incarnation of the devil, as if you have betrayed them with poor play.

The only people you can truly rely on are friends—those who have proven their loyalty before your fame. They are the ones who are there even when you blow a chance to put the team into the Top 10. They remind you that no matter how well you may have played, in the end we're all nothing but dust.

That lesson became painfully clear my senior year in a game against Ohio State. It was game in which I couldn't hit the broad side of a barn from point blank range. I missed four foul shots in the closing minutes of the second half, and we lost by a single bucket. In the shower, I hid my tears in the water jets.

After almost every game, throngs of students waited for me as I exited the arena. They usually wanted to shake my hand, congratulate me, or make a comment on the game. ("Nice dunk, dude!" and the like.) After this disaster, only my true friends—point guard Danny Earl; Nate Althouse, a walk-on team hero; Salima Davidson, the All-American volleyball star; and my fellow

Star Trek fanatic, Dennis Shafnisky—were there for me. It was autumn, and the leaves shuffled under our feet on the stone paths as we walked in silence back to the dorms together.

●••

The good will generated by helping get Penn State on the basketball map had gotten me the proverbial key to the city. And I vowed to open every door I came across. I hung out with Paterno; I got to know the Penn State president, Joab Thomas; I'd peek into the coach's office and chat with Bruce. If I wanted to meet with Joab or Tim Curley, the athletic director, about student-athlete affairs (or anything else, for that matter), I could get onto their calendars. I helped organize a group of student-athletes to speak at local schools. I was made a member of Skull and Bones, the fraternal society made famous (or pointless) by President Bush's membership.

I made so many appearances at events and classrooms across Happy Valley that I developed an inspirational stock speech extolling the notion of striving, loosely based on what I'd learned since coming up with The Plan. Young people are often told in various ways to accept their lot. They grow up believing they can't aspire to anything more than minimum wage and the night shift. Rural folk sometimes think the best they can do is a farm subsidy. Urban kids rebel when they are led to believe they can't go beyond fry cook.

"Look, I'm playing a game, whether or not I succeed, that many people said was impossible," I explained to my young audiences. "If I can accomplish my goal—a fat, awkward kid from Manchester, where many people don't know what basketball is— so can every single person in this room."

I'm not sure how much the message sunk in. But it certainly helped me articulate my own goals. It was another audience that would expect me to live up to my word.

I went to places where people never thought a Penn State ballplayer would set foot. I took great pleasure in blowing away their preconceptions of athletes, especially black athletes.

After one speech to an entirely white suburban audience, a middle-aged woman remarked, "I didn't think you'd be so articulate." In other words, she'd expected a dumb nigger.

Yet, I was gratified at the way in which white audiences reacted to me when I ventured into more rural areas of the state. Given my own stereotypes about country folk, I expected a bunch of "hicks" who would never get involved with the likes of me. Yet all these little white kids treated me like a king.

I'm nothing but a bigoted idiot, I said to myself. *I can't ask other people to drop their assumptions if I hold onto mine.*

Of course, not everyone could be redeemed. When I was out on the streets at night, looking after my kids, cars would pass and slow down. Then the window would open and someone would stick their head out and scream, "Meeeccchhhh!" I'd wave and laugh; it was all in good fun. But one night a car pulled up as usual. I started to raise my hand to waive when instead of my name, I heard the word "nigger!", angry and loud. The car then sped off, burning rubber, the coward's approach to spreading fear.

The episode put me in a contemplative mood. Here I was, the best basketball player this campus had ever seen. I worked with kids, treated everyone with respect, worked my hardest to be a good citizen in a town that had welcomed me warmly. But to some people, no matter how hard I tried or how many games I won, I'd always be nothing more than a nigger.

One afternoon in Rec Hall during my junior year, I noticed a tall, good-looking guy I recognized as a member of the volleyball team. He was wandering around, somewhat aimlessly, occasionally glancing at me.

Even with all my homo-innocence, I could interpret longing. I was shocked that such a handsome guy would show an interest in me. I followed him upstairs to the bathroom, where he motioned for me to follow him into one of the stalls.

I didn't have to be Sherlock Holmes to figure out what to do next. Cruising is intuitive, and the fact that I'd noticed four legs in a stall instead of two when I'd used the bathroom earlier was a pretty good clue.

I debated turning around.

What on earth would happen if someone walked in? I certainly could not afford a sex scandal. I'd achieved a certain public status in the intimate world of a college campus; I had so much to lose. If my secret got out, my career was dead. There was nothing in The Plan to deal with a sexual crisis, except to infer that it was not a good idea—not a good idea at all.

I didn't count a single gay person among my friends or acquaintances. The only images of homoeroticism on campus were ludicrous: the antics of frat boys, infamous for meting out to pledges a combination of naked spankings, tea bagging (an obscene act that has nothing to do with my favorite beverage), and other activities straight men fantasize that gay guys enjoy.

There was only one gay bar in the area, Chumley's on West College Avenue. I'd never seen the inside of it, partly because I was scared to walk through the door and partly because its windows were darkened—a telling metaphor for the closet that in a way matched my own precarious cover.

CHAPTER II ●●●] Blue

Though I understood why the windows were darkened, it was a disquieting sight nonetheless. What does it say about a society in which a significant minority feels it necessary to go to such lengths to conceal their very identities?

By the early 1990s in big American cities, the gay rights movement was in full bloom. But it was a far cry from small town Pennsylvania. My image of homosexuality came from frat houses and the freaky leather Blue Oyster Club bar in the movie *Police Academy.*

Although I was unaware of it at the time, the women's basketball coach, Rene Portland, had allegedly been purging lesbians from her team for years (an endless task in women's basketball), a policy that would have only succeeded in driving away open lesbians, not all lesbians. If the allegations are true, she was willing (and some say she remains willing) to demonize the very athletes she depends upon to do her job. Even her wins were tarnished by bigotry.

Portland might feel some kind of moral prerogative, but the way I felt in college about my sexuality was nothing less than a form of torment, a booming tinnitus and blinding light all around as I tried to study and play and do good works.

The closest thing to any revelation in the basketball world at the time came from Magic Johnson, when he announced that he was HIV positive. Magic, however, made it abundantly clear he didn't get HIV from same-sex activities. In fact, the subtext of the whole episode was that being considered gay is worse than acknowledging that he'd been with multiple women, sometimes at the same time. Even then, it was hard to understand how a serial philanderer of that magnitude—or any magnitude—would be considered, by right-wing Christian standards, any less of a sinner than a gay person who has little or no sex at all, even if that was about to change.

●●●

Back at the men's room, probity lost out to passion, and before long I found myself in lip lock with the tall young man in a space barely big enough to contain one.

This is where the scene mostly fades to black. Let's just say it was not the most romantic of encounters. It wasn't sex, exactly, that went on in there. Fully clothed, it was more like a lot of nervous fumbling. Imagine fitting two people, one nearly seven feet tall, into that three-by-four stall, and you'll see what I mean.

What lingered for me was not the sex, which, except for being my first experience, was forgettable. It was the kissing. For days I could still taste the salty sweetness of his tongue, which seemed to have an almost chemical charge when it touched mine. Instantly I could see why kissing girls had been such a failure, and why I was so fascinated by the wrestlers whom I'd caught kissing in secret back in high school.

So many guys in similarly anonymous situations refuse that form of intimacy, as if to say that any affection would be an admission that this was a gay experience rather than simply a sexual one—like a couple of frat guys just getting off.

More than anything, it was the kiss that told me what I had denied I was. Or at least who I hoped to become some day when it became possible to have so much more than a quickie in the loo.

I kept returning, so these encounters must have done something for me, fulfilling a nascent longing to be touched, recognized, deemed attractive. They were some confusing combination of fervent, sordid, disquieting, and thrilling all at the same time.

Looking back, they also served as a relief from the grinding daily pressure of expectations, particularly my own. That they were not part of The Plan—in fact, they were contrary to it, and that made them even more alluring.

I never hated myself; my desire for other men felt as natural as my right-handedness. It was simply incompatible with how I'd defined myself at the time, with whom I'd become on campus.

In a hot shower scrubbing away the evidence afterward, I repeated to myself, over and over, I can't be *the* basketball player and *this* man who likes other men in this way. *I can't be this man I am.*

Looking back, it didn't make any sense. I lacked the knowledge, wisdom, and support to reconcile these parts of myself that seemed so disparate, even though it is now so obvious to me that they are one and the same. The notion of uttering the word "gay" and my name in the same sentence was simply preposterous. So I went around pretending it was a problem that didn't exist. In fact, I told myself my subterfuge was working, until I happened across some graffiti scrawled on the Rec Hall locker room: "AMAECHI'S A BIG FAG."

Quite literally true, but unkind and rather shocking nonetheless. I'd taken some chances once in awhile, and apparently someone had noticed. I had not been quite as discrete as I'd imagined. Fortunately for me, the epithet was surrounded by other scribbled comments to the effect of, "Great guy, role model, terrific ballplayer," etc. So I simply rubbed out the anti-gay remark and left the rest, reflecting my approach to the question of my sexuality.

●●●

In the short story "Am I Blue?", Bruce Coville writes about a teenager tormented by his sexuality until, magically, all the gay people at his high school, from the class bully to the PE teacher, turn an identifiable shade of blue. Overnight, discrimination ends and everyone lives happily ever after.

It's a bit utopian, of course. Look no further than the various shades of black, brown, and yellow to know that skin color can also draw discrimination. Nonetheless, there were times when I couldn't help but fantasize about that kind of miracle at Penn State.

One day I was shooting hoops in the gym when I needed to use the bathroom for, well, more ordinary purposes. I pushed opened the door and a member of the training staff had his hands on the front of the stall with a wide grin on his face. The act was underneath him, behind the stall, out of sight.

When he saw me, the look of pleasure turned to shock and then horror, as if he was going to drop dead right there. I knew exactly what was going through his head because it could just as easily have been me: *I've just been outed to the captain of the basketball team. My career is over.*

I resolved to put him at ease. The next time I saw this good man, in the training room, he avoided eye contact. So I included him in a joke, making a point of looking him in the eye, signalling he was okay by me. I could literally see him breathing a sigh of relief. He responded by treating me like he always had, providing an ice pack for my aching back and tending to my other ailments.

It was all such a cruel joke. I recognized guys from the wrestling team, from track, from all over school (especially from volleyball!), even another basketball player. We were all an invisible shade of blue. To acknowledge one another and our minority status threatened doom—unless there was some way we could coordinate our message. And that's exactly what discrimination prevented.

In some ways, we were inadvertently fulfilling society's expectations. By denying gay people recognition not only of who they are but also of their relationships, we sometimes ended up having the kinds of illicit sex that fit the stereotype. By banning marriage, our marginalization is further ensured. Political conservatives tend to define gay people as "immoral," "perverted," and "promiscuous," yet they deny them the one institution that to them represents the opposite. It's a handy catch-22 with which to bind a whole group of people to second-class citizenship.

Straight people have sex in bathroom stalls (in England they do it in parking lots so other straight couples can watch —it's called "dogging"). Gay people have sex in bathroom stalls. It's not the sexiest location in the world. But gay people often feel they have little choice, as they are often denied the opportunity to date openly.

All over campus and off, students were having sex like bunnies. Nobody said a word when boys came out of girls' dorm rooms in the morning, towel wrapped around the waist, on the way to the shower. Back then (though perhaps not today), it would have created a minor outrage to discover a boy coming out of another boy's room in what should really be nothing more than just another collegiate rite of passage.

CHAPTER 12 ●●●] # If the Son Is a Star

Toward the beginning of junior year, I picked up the phone to hear a somber tone I'd hadn't heard since the death of my grandmother.

"John, are you alone?" Mum asked.

She told me that her breast cancer, which she had fought off eight years ago, had returned. "This time it's not going away."

I'd never felt so utterly alone. Memories of moments we'd spent together washed over me, and I regretted that I hadn't cherished every single one. The sorrow mocked my achievements, many of which I'd accomplished for her. Everything felt hollow.

When she was first diagnosed, I'd stifled a laugh when she told me she would undergo a mastectomy. The girls, in shock, quite naturally wailed and cried and wailed and cried some more.

I was embarrassed at my reaction, until I realized it was because of the absurdity of the notion that my mother, as iron-willed and physically strong as two men combined, must have part of her removed to save her life. I could not have imagined a more ludicrous plot on TV.

She had rebounded impressively from that operation. The prognosis was good. Permanent remission was a strong possibility.

But this time it was no joke, and it was I who bawled on the phone with her and for hours afterward. I cried because she was brave. I cried when she told me I couldn't come home, that I needed to stay, play, and excel. How could she think about a game at a time like this? She was dying, yet her concern was for her son's future.

It took me forever to hang up. I feared that when the connection went dead, it would be the last time I'd ever hear her voice. I knew she had more time—the doctors had given her a year or so—but I'd reverted to a little boy, fearing the loss of my mother's embrace.

My life at Penn State had not changed materially. But I wandered through my routine like a zombie. Everything was off. Days were longer, nights restless, practices and schoolwork harder, games more punishing.

I had never before realized the mutability of reality. One day you have a clear focus, and the next you are lost in a haze of uncertainty, wondering why you are where you are.

I usually spent most of my time at Rec Hall, a sort of second home. With no idea where to go or what to do next, I sat in the bleachers, adjacent to the coaches' offices, looking down at the "lunch bunch," a group of professors and grad students playing ball.

Ordinarily I would have joined in. Now I felt nothing but contempt for the game. It all seemed pointless, players battling the infirmities of their own bodies as much as one another. What could possibly come of all that running and jumping? Arguing over fouls, throwing elbows, limping off the court—it was as if they were flaunting their frivolous behavior at me.

I started to cry all over again, right there in blue seats. Mum was dying, thousands of miles away, and here I was stuck watching people playing a silly game, a game in which I'd invested everything, only to have it take me away from the person who'd made it possible.

Over the next days and weeks, I'd gone from focused, energetic, and intense to unresponsive, lazy, and without purpose. I could have cared less about class, which I skipped. In practice, always a source of great pride, I went through the motions.

Finally, I walked to the office of my academic advisor, Sandy, and closed the door behind me. The sorrows poured forth. When I was done, she gave me a big hug, and the instant she touched me I knew I had an ally in my struggle to become number 13 again.

During our last conversation, Mum said she *needed* me to write to her, to help her stay strong. It was the least I could do. I took paper and pen to Rec Hall to compose my post-apocalyptic letter. Listening to Sting croon, just as I had when I had first left Manchester for the States, I wanted to tell her how much I would miss her, how I wondered how to carry on without her.

As I listened through my headphones, it became clear that verse would be the best way to express all these raw, confusing emotions. I haven't the foggiest idea whether what I wrote was any good, only that it meant a lot to me and, I hoped, to Mum. The result was *If the Son Is a Star.* It's a bit epic, so I'll just quote one stanza:

The Sun is a star
the torch that is passed
spirits that are one
together at last
knowledge more than was told
words felt
not heard
a flame that inspired
healed not burnt

A few days later, Coach called me into his office. This wasn't unusual. Bruce and I talked a lot since my first conversation with him on a recruiting visit, outside his office in the bleachers. I'd become the original coffee thief at Rec Hall, moving from office to office, including his, filling my cup (no doubt an NCAA violation of some sort). Apparently, Mum had called to explain her illness and to warn Bruce that I might be out of sorts. I fessed up to struggling. Like Sandy, he promised to be there for me, no matter what. I had thought I was getting a grip, but then I broke down yet again, and the man some said had the emotional life of a stone gave me a bear hug.

After my visits with Sandy and Coach, my life gradually regained a sense of normalcy. Yet I can't say I've truly been the same since. In nightmares, I still picture myself as a surviving child in an old war photograph, looking at the camera in wide-eyed shock, clinging desperately to the body of a dead parent.

I derived strength from my Mum, and even in her illness, she was a source of inspiration. I had to work, to strive, to achieve, because I was my mother's son. In her death, rather than retreat from the world, I vowed to carry on in her memory.

She could no longer shine, but that meant I would shine all the brighter for us both. It seemed a daunting task to inherit, but I soon realized it was a task she had carefully prepared me to tackle. The Plan, after all, was so much more than a document. It was her wisdom, handed down to me in document form.

As soon as I regained my composure, I turned my attention to saying goodbye. Christmas would be the last opportunity for the entire family to be together. Equally, I wanted to make sure Mum could rest assured that I had, and would, make it. So I knew she had to come see me play one last time.

I asked Coach about missing the Bethune Cookman game before the Big Ten season started. He agreed, even though we both knew it could hurt the team's preparation. He had recruited a lot of new talent that year, and there were expectations that were unlikely to be met without my full participation.

My teammates were even more adamant. "What are you waiting for," said Matt Gaudio, though as my backup I suspected an ulterior motive.

It was decided that rather than slink off into the night, I should make a statement in the regular pregame press conference about my departure. The media had anointed us a serious contender, and the coverage was nonstop. A twisted ankle was considered newsworthy. After my last game before leaving, I showered, dressed, and scurried to the pressroom.

I usually felt comfortable among reporters, and they with me (I give great quote!), but this was the first time I had to talk about something so intimate and heart wrenching, something that had nothing to do with the game. Jeff Brewer, our press officer, who had become a friend, announced that I had something to say, and then left.

I looked around the room that day and saw familiar faces. This time I felt as if I were naked, revealing personal information to a crowd used to seeing athletes express little but confidence and invincibility. The last thing I wanted was to shed more tears as the cameras rolled. I choked out my message, and hurried out, heading to catch a ride to JFK airport in New York.

Danny, Nate, Salima, and Dennis accompanied me. As I was driven through the night, I listed to old Christmas tunes in a desperate attempt to get me in the mood for the holiday that I'd forever associate with the loss of my mother.

●●●

A wave of relief swept over me at the Manchester airport when I was greeted by Muriel and Uki.

Entering the house, it seemed as if I'd never left, and I regressed to the days when Mum's existence seemed permanent. I hugged her for a long time, not quite grasping how someone could be both in my arms and not long for the world at the same time.

There was a comforting continuity. The Christmas tree was in the same place it had always been, with the same ornaments, cards displayed neatly on the mantle. Mum made the same meal, turkey with all the trimmings, followed by a desert of trifle, a sinful combination of jelly, custard, sponge cake, cream, and alcohol.

Mum was nothing if not exacting, working to take the uncertainty out of even the worst situation. She informed me in no uncertain terms that I was not to sacrifice academically or athletically for her. She practically ordered me to regain my focus.

I was not to come back again. She made sure that in my short stay, we talked mostly about the future—*my* future. But as I sat in my familiar place at the end of her bed in the dark, all I wanted to talk about was the past.

There were a million questions flooding my mind, from practical to philosophical, that I'd never have the chance to ask her.

●●●

When I got back to campus, everyone, including play-by-play announcers live on the air, sent good wishes to me and Mum. I sent her the tapes so she could hear the outpouring of goodwill.

Even other players and coaches from Big Ten teams sent their regards. Before a home game at Penn State, Bobby Knight took me aside, complimenting me not only on the improvement of my play, but on the grace with which he thought I was handling the difficult circumstances. It was the sweet side of the great coach that he rarely lets others see.

I appreciated the sentiment, but I didn't feel particularly graceful, on or off the court. Basketball was suddenly hard again, and it showed. I don't know what caused our somewhat lackluster season. Perhaps it was my distraction, though I played well enough to win a bunch of honors. Bruce had brought in a lot of new talent, but that succeeded mostly in making us better players and not a better team.

The prized recruit was a six-foot-eight forward from Syracuse named Glenn Sekunda. The hope was that we would be a potent one-two punch, eliminating my double teams. There was no questioning his ability. He was mobile, versatile, and a terrific shooter.

Sekunda's attitude that year left a lot to be desired, though. It became clear that he was just waiting for me to graduate so that my team would become his, an extremely selfish attitude for which I think the team paid dearly.

We performed better when the Big Ten games rolled around. But we never quite had the team unity or grit to get to the next level, to compete for that elusive Penn State basketball title.

The individual awards poured in: First Team Academic All-America, First Team All Big Ten. Yet I'd never been more aware that the sport, like life, is a team game, and a lot of guys mistakenly believed they could show their stuff and that the victories would come "next time" around. For the first time in my still young life I *knew* for a fact that more often than not there *isn't* a next time. The only time is now.

●●●

Mum was gravely ill when she came to visit me toward the end of my junior year in 1993, the only time she saw me play college ball. This was before it was easy to get any television channel anywhere in the world, simply piped in over the Internet, cable, or satellite.

She stayed at a local hotel. She was so frail I was afraid she wouldn't last the trip. By being at her side, I did my best to assuage the primal fear that she had alleviated in so many patients over the years. We spent a lot of time in the atrium restaurant just talking and being together. She steered the conversation toward my friends, my life, my aspirations.

I was desperate to assure her, through my play, that my future in the game was bright and that there was no need to worry. Over the years, she'd learned a great deal more about the game than she probably wanted to know, and she would be able to tell just by observing.

She was in the stands when we took on Wisconsin at home, where, perhaps trying too hard, I played poorly.

The next game, against Minnesota, was her last chance to see me play before returning to Manchester. So I played the game like it was my last. I literally secured the victory by myself, a rebounding, shot-blocking, scoring menace. Even for a highly motivated athlete, I was ablaze that night with passion to excel, and it showed. I was superb.

In hindsight, Mum was rightfully more concerned about my soul than my play. "It's great John's doing what he wants to do and getting an opportunity to do it," she told a local newspaper at about this time. "But I told him what I'm most proud of is that, even when it's cold and snowing, if a little kid runs up, John takes his gloves off and shakes his hand. He takes time to talk. I think he's going to be all right."

The day before she flew home, I skipped class to have breakfast with her again. I was describing mentoring a troubled but promising kid named Jose. "See that woman over there, that's Jose's mom," I told her.

"Have you spoken to her?" she asked. "Mothers love to talk about their sons. She can be a big help to you." It brought tears to my eyes. She was not only talking about Jose's mom. She was referring to her pride in talking about me.

Earlier, she'd sent me a silver chalice. "To my son in whom I am well pleased," it was inscribed, quoting scripture. Of course it was an ironic reference, perhaps a sly nod to what some might call my savior complex, but the message itself could not have been more genuine.

●••

In March of 1995, my final year of college, we reached the final four at the National Invitation Tournament. I drew a tough assignment in the early rounds, seven-foot-two Constantine Popa, nearly half a foot taller than me. It was great to find myself on the court with bigger, rather than smaller, people—another benefit of my newfound occupation.

I had played against plenty of big men by then, but Popa was extraordinarily tall and I could not exactly out-big this big man. Bruce Lee famously insisted that you shouldn't box a boxer or wrestle a wrestler. In other words, don't try to outplay an opponent at what they do best, because you will get your ass kicked.

I didn't try to go over his lanky frame. Instead, I used my strength and leverage to bully him into submission and my quickness to go around him. I torched him for 25 points.

But with the notable exception of the Popa game, I labored under a barrage of double teams, lost in a sea of defenders. It was my friend, the point guard Danny Earl, who did us proud, earning all-tournament honors.

The burden of Mum's illness was still with me. Every time I was on the court, I wanted to honor her with my play. Yet it was hard to maintain the level of enthusiasm of the Minnesota game. When I did not play well, I was letting down not just my team but my mother as well.

I spent weeks languishing—skipping class, sleeping, and eating everything in sight. I ended up needing to work myself into tip-top shape for critical pre-NBA draft camps.

I bought my first car at the age of 22, in time for my senior year. It was a forest green Grand Cherokee, the beginning of my love affair with the automobile. It was one of the few cars in which I could sit comfortably in the driver's seat.

I'd drive through the mountains, taking in the panoramic views of Nittany Valley, blasting Seal. There was something soothing about the hum of the engine and the solitude of the landscape, a feeling that if anything would be permanent in my life, it would be my ability to enjoy moments like this.

●●●

In the spring of 1994, I got a call from Muriel urging me to "get home as soon as possible." Mum was fading, and this was my last chance to say goodbye. (I missed the end of classes, but every teacher except one allowed me to make up the work. I got an F in softball, of all things, for not showing up. The basketball star had failed softball!)

I found Mum in bed and fading, but, as usual, in control of everything. She'd already made the funeral arrangements and paid for everything, in advance. She made sure her will and legal issues were in order. There was nothing for us to do but grieve.

I sat on the edge of her bed, holding her hand. As she faded in and out of consciousness, she mostly tried to console me, as usual, and didn't really want to talk about the past. I had too many questions at that point to start grilling her, anyway. I just wanted to be with her.

I'll never forget the gasping sound her lungs made. She was dying from breast cancer, but it had spread to her lungs. Years of smoking didn't help. I tell parents who smoke that the last thing they want to do is leave their kids with memories of that sound—strained breathing as the lungs literally melt away—as their lasting, searing memory of a dying parent. I still hear it in my nightmares.

Just before she died, three days later, in May, at the age of 50, Mum gave me a present that she forbade me to open until my birthday, seven months later.

I opened it on my 23rd birthday, the following November. It turned out to be a silver Native American dream catcher to ward off the nightmares.

She knew there would be plenty of those to come.

CHAPTER 13 ●●●] Twinkies

Of all the things that might slow or derail The Plan, the Twinkie was an unlikely suspect, especially since I didn't even discover this all-American delicacy until 1995, my senior year at Penn State. It was a diabolical new twist on an old nemesis: sweets.

Even as my play remained solid, I struggled emotionally at the end of my college career. Mum's death still weighed heavily—and so did all those Twinkies. I loved their spongy richness, and I devoured them by the dozen.

They call it senioritis, not a malaise I ever expected to suffer. In my last semester, I consumed everything college towns abundantly offer, from junk food to pizza to Alabama Slammers that I downed with my buddy Dennis at Gingerbread Man.

I moped, piled on 20 pounds of fat, and put too much stock in my college stats. I played plenty of pick-up ball, but I lost what had become a trademark: my ability to practice in a way that best replicated the game itself, against good opponents, working on useful skills. I stopped doing the strenuous drills and exercises that would have kept me sharp while working off the Twinkies. Every day I made seemingly small but bad decisions that were adding up to one very big problem.

A little slacking off would have been expected—and I have to say richly deserved. I'd accomplished a lot, on and off the court. Many of my classmates, after all, had already purchased their Eurail passes, images of Eiffel Tower romances dancing in their heads.

But for a guy on the NBA fast track, it was a risky lapse. I was only human, but that wasn't good enough in a time when I needed to maintain a machine-like intensity.

My court exploits had gone to my head. Senior year, I averaged 16.1 points and 9.9 rebounds per game while becoming the second player in Penn State history to record 1,300 points and 700 rebounds over an entire college career.

I was named big this, all that, all everything.

Believing my own hype, I imagined that everything I wanted would follow automatically. Comfortable with the idea that I was good—*really* good—for the first time since I'd started playing, I promptly took my eye off the ball.

●●●

At the Plymouth Invitational Tournament, a pre-draft camp for NBA prospects where you are poked and prodded like prized pigs, I played like one. I was so out of shape that I could barely keep up with the pace of play, let alone show off the skills I'd so assiduously developed.

For the first time since I'd tangled with Eddie Fogler at Vanderbilt, The Plan was in serious trouble. There was a possibility I might not get drafted at all. And you could count on one hand the number of guys who made it in the NBA without being drafted in the first few rounds.

I needed a crack agent to steer me through a thicket that just got thicker. Fortunately, Plymouth also happened to be the place where agents made their full-court press on collegiate players. They went after promising athletes like Dennis Rodman chasing a loose ball. Luckily, I was still a commodity in these circles, still thought of as NBA-worthy.

Thanks to ESPN's chronicling of my dedication to the area's youth, I was well known not only as a standout college ballplayer, but also as a rather unusual one, one with "character."

I was wined and dined by a procession of smooth talkers. Like finding a college coach, the trick was to differentiate the good agents from the good bullshit artists.

I settled on Bill Sweek of Los Angeles and his colleague, Kenny Grant, who worked with European players. Before becoming an agent, Bill had played alongside Lew Alcindor for John Wooden at UCLA. With a warm smile and salt-and-pepper hair, he came across as both wise and low-key, hardly the Jerry McGuire stereotype.

Bill had done his homework. He knew I wasn't stupid, and by avoiding promises he couldn't keep, he came across as resourceful and realistic about how he could help me. He knew my game inside and out, an asset in finding me the right home to build a career. We laid out a strategy to get me back into NBA form. I had only one more chance to prove myself, at another pre-draft camp, the Desert Classic in Phoenix. The camp had already filled up, but Bill wrangled me a spot.

I had one month to work off the Twinkies and get into NBA-training camp shape, the challenge of a lifetime in what was starting to seem like a lifetime of challenges. I longed for something, anything, to come easily.

At least I would not be on my own. Bill set me up with—and paid for—a world-class trainer, Warren Anderson, to help guide my conditioning.

Warren let me know up front that he required one thing: massive amounts of hard work. He didn't put up with clients, no matter how lucrative, who were unwilling to put in the effort. He wasn't going to stand over your shoulder, screaming like a maniacal drill sergeant. Any gains his clients got from such an approach would be lost once his contract ended anyway. *You* supplied the motivation and discipline; he provided the oversight, training, and technique. I had drive to spare, and, despising the very notion of negative motivation, we were a good combination.

My days were identical. Up at 7 a.m. for tea and a light breakfast. By 9, I was on a grassy field sprinting and running through agility, quickness, and balance drills until I ached. Then I'd head to Coffee Plantation at the Scottsdale Biltmore for soup and salad, and back to the gym with Warren, where I'd lift weights for one to two hours and work on core exercises. This was the worst part of the regimen—nothing but the grinding monotony of intense physical pain.

Warren—and every player I've ever spoken to—believes that it's good to be both strong and agile, but not too tight. Any motion on the floor that resembles a bench press is likely to draw a whistle. In other words, you don't have to look like David Robinson to be as effective as David Robinson.

The evenings found me at one of the valley's LA Fitness Sports Clubs, squaring off against the likes of Richard Jefferson, Donovan McNabb (who is also an excellent basketball player), and Mike Bibby. It was critical that I match up with the best, rather than the usual wannabes you might find on any given night at a regular gym. To a man, they were tremendous athletes, in top shape, and just being on the same court, competing, gave me a shot in the arm as I headed into the Desert Classic.

Warren did his best to help me undo the damage I'd done to myself. But by the time the Classic rolled around, I was hardly classic Amaechi. I was quicker and thinner, and everyone who saw me at the Plymouth Invitational commented on how much better I looked.

At the hotel where the league put me up, I roomed with Greg Ostertag, a loveable mountain of a man from the University of Kansas who made me feel small. I sat with Greg watching television as letters from teams were pushed under the door.

They were all addressed to Greg, asking him to come in for interviews. It made perfect sense. At seven-foot-two, he was a natural center, and he was playing well. I needed to show off a range of skills, not something I could do without being in better shape.

But that didn't stop me from daydreaming that just one letter would have my name on it—something that was not to be.

●●•

The day of the 1996 NBA draft, I sat in Randy and Judy's living room back in Toledo watching it unfold on TV. It was nice to be in the company of old friends, and we tried to make light of the situation as we drank beer and munched on chips.

Although I'd never expected to be a high first-rounder, a lot of experts said I'd go in the low first or high second.

Here's how one astute scout had me rated:

"John's work ethic has made up for a lack of tremendous athletic ability. He uses his big body very well, and has a complete arsenal of post moves that make him very dangerous. He can hit medium range jump shots and has shown the potential to make longer shots, although he was discouraged from moving away from the basket at Penn State.

"As a college player, he was basically unguardable one-on-one. This led to double teams, which he struggled with. His passing improved steadily, but still needs work. His ball handling is not on par with better NBA power forwards, his natural pro position. These problems, I imagine, are ones which John will be able to work on and improve. His lack of speed means he'll never be much of a full-court NBA player, although he does work hard, and so is often in on the tail end of fast breaks."

There was enough positive in that assessment to put me in play. But the return of my baby fat meant my phone might not ring on draft day, potentially costing me as much as $2 million.

I watched nervously as a procession of familiar names— Lorenzen Wright, Erick Dampier, Vitaly Potapenko—went up on the board. I knew these guys because I'd kicked their asses. I didn't resent them getting their due. But I had no doubt my name should have been alongside theirs.

The writing was on the wall: I'd earned the dreaded appellation—un-drafted free agent. My career hadn't even started and I was already embarking on a comeback.

Bill assured me all was not lost. Big men were always in short supply. Plenty of teams would be on the lookout for last-minute bargains. If I spent a few more months with Warren, he was confident he could find me a team in time for training camp in October.

I returned again to Toledo, where I'd left much of my stuff—including my Jeep Cherokee—at Randy and Judy's after leaving Penn State. This time I'd have to get myself back out to Phoenix, no easy chore because I'd already run up $35,000 in credit card debt, a sum I could only easily repay with a pro contract, any pro contract. Jerry helped me pack the Jeep with all my possessions and drove with me across the country.

Once in Phoenix, I rented a run-down, furnished, one-bedroom efficiency, sleeping on a bare mattress under a green crocheted blanket. An air conditioner dripped foul water all night. I rented a TV so I'd have something to do as I rested between workouts.

Bill managed to get me a tryout with a team in Greece, which I promptly failed. But before I was to fly back to the States, he got me a two-game $10,000 contract with Pitch Cholet in France, which needed a fill-in for an injured player. The money helped get me through the rest of the summer.

Back in Phoenix, my workouts were going well, honing me into something more closely approximating NBA shape. The key now was to find the club that was most likely to provide a tryout and that was lacking big-man depth. The stakes were high. If we guessed wrong, I'd go through training camp before being cut, making it hard to find a club at a time when rosters had largely been filled.

Bill and I sat up late several nights scanning rosters. We settled on Cleveland, a promising young team whose best big man, Brad Dougherty, was injured. Also, Hot Rod Williams had been traded.

The Cavaliers invited me to camp at Gund Arena, putting me up at the Renaissance Hotel across the street with a bunch of other players. The franchise threw in a few thousand bucks in appearance money. They were right to assume that most of us were pretty much broke. It was a camp for long-shots, but we were of no use if we were out hustling up spare change for dinner rather than resting and replenishing our energy with decent meals.

When I walked into camp, head coach Mike Fratello immediately marched up to me. And I do mean *up*. Fratello was all of five-foot-seven, but he made up for his size with his outsized personality, the necessity of a small man in a game of giants.

"John, what have you done?" he asked, incredulously. "I swear you've lost 50 pounds."

He must have seen me in my Twinkie phase at the pre-draft workouts.

The truth is that I was in exponentially better condition than when he'd seen me last. I'd done enough cardio to slim down and enough weights to tone up. I hadn't lost 50 pounds, but I was happy to let him believe I had.

"Perception is reality," Warren kept reminding me. At his urging, I got daily massages designed to lengthen my muscles so they would *look* better in stretching drills. He had me sit in the scorching Phoenix sun, my skin turning a darker shade of brown. Coaches, he insisted, often unconsciously relate darker skin both to health and better athleticism, based in part on prejudices that favored black athletes. He also made the point that if I looked better, I would also feel better and play better, too.

In the process, I racked up the first of a few career trivia quiz facts. The Cavs TV announcer, Michael Reghi (who used to cover my high school games as a sports reporter in Toledo, Ohio), informed me that I was the first undrafted player in NBA history to start in an opening game. I suspect that by telling me this, he was trying to help propel me through what he knew would be a gruelling season.

In another preseason game a few days later against Boston, I fouled out relatively early and thought nothing of it. The rookie fouled out. So what?

After the game, Fratello was not happy. "We are relying on you to play big minutes," he said. "You can't foul out." This was the Michigan ankle twist all over again—a reminder that I was a bigger factor than I'd assumed.

I was trying to do too much. Cage spent a lot of extra time with me that season, kindly advising me on how to break down the game and make it more manageable. Rather than go into a game thinking I had to get eight rebounds and only three fouls, he suggested I set goals for each quarter.

Now I would go into a game thinking short term: *This quarter I'll try for two boards and to waste only one foul, but only if I have to.* The lesson was that in basketball, as in life, you have to do what you can *in the moment.*

Cage made it look easy. He was a rebounding, shot-blocking force of nature, and I was merely a sponge for his wisdom. He had a natural talent that he supplemented with a well-honed mental approach. I mostly lacked the first and was in a desperate search for the second.

●••

I had made it, signing a one-year, non-guaranteed deal for the NBA minimum of $250,000. This is what I'd worked six years to achieve. I'd gone from overweight oaf and wretched freak to one of the top 300 basketball players in the world.

The most important thing wasn't even getting there. It was coming through on my promise to Mum, to Joe, to many others. And to myself.

But I wasn't celebrating. Exhausted by the effort, I was secretly afraid to upset the karmic balance by getting happy and satisfied.

I rented a $900 two-bedroom apartment in Westlake, a suburb about five miles from Gund Arena in central Cleveland. I lived there alone for about three months before Uki, following her acting dreams to America, moved in. She had been a stage actor in the UK, and was hoping to find a foothold in the U.S. market. Granted, Cleveland wasn't the acting capital of the West. But it was a practical start because she could live with me for free and branch out from there.

It was the first time I'd lived with my own family since moving to the States, so it was a treat. We cooked, watched TV, and reminisced about the old days, about Mum. She knew not the slightest thing about basketball, so being with her was like a vacation from the game.

In my down time I volunteered at Westlake High School, which was thrilled to have any Cavalier around—even unheralded me. There I mentored Tom, a scrawny kid who was rebelling against the conformity he saw all around him. The rebellion, however, was only hurting him, as his grades were failing and he was struggling. He was never a "bad" kid, he just needed a little guidance, structure, and support.

By that point, I'd had enough mentoring experience to size a kid up pretty accurately. I could tell that he was desperate for someone he trusted, other than his parents, to tell him that he could be something special if he would only focus.

I tried to get the point across in as many ways as possible. I finally told him about the dangers of ending up a Silverfish, those tiny, unremarkable sea creatures that mass anonymously into a protective ball when they feel the vibrations of predators. It's a great survival instinct but not a thriving instinct. The world needs Silverfish. They are an important part of the food chain. But if Tom moved through life on his current path, he could expect nothing more than a pretty anonymous life.

Today Tom is no Silverfish, having made himself into a successful businessman in Chicago. I'd like to believe he would have sorted himself out without me, and he surely would have, but it is also gratifying to think I may have played a role.

My experience with Tom, and the power I had as a ballplayer to get through to him, was far more rewarding than the trappings of my still precarious career. It was so illuminating that it made me think even more about having my own kids—a goal that between basketball and my major secret was going to be a challenge.

With my first paychecks, I paid off the 35 grand of debt. Meanwhile, my teammates playfully deemed me lacking in NBA style, and Chris Mills gave me a box full of size-15 alligator skin shoes, a perfect fit. Taking the hint, I bought two tailored suits for the road and had a couple of pairs of European-style jeans made, but that was about it. I was hardly going on a spending spree with my future still in doubt. In the back of my mind, I fully expected to need the money to pay for graduate school in psychology.

The Cavs' veterans took me under their wings, mercifully refraining from rookie hazing—a game I would not have tolerated. They slapped me around when I had my head up my ass on the court and picked me up when I was down.

Dan Majerle, he of the sweet jumper, treated me to dinner at Lawson's Steakhouse in downtown Chicago, where we drank good wine and I listened as he imparted his knowledge about shooting and making your mark among the best.

The pro locker room was the most flamboyant place I'd ever been this side of a swanky club full of martini-drinking gay men. Chris' alligator shoes were the least of it. The guys flaunted their perfect bodies. They bragged of their sexual exploits. They checked out each other's cocks. They primped in front of the mirror, applying cologne and hair gel by the bucketful.

Some guys just lacked self-consciousness. Others clearly liked to show off. I can't blame them: If I had three percent body fat, I'd probably flaunt it too.

One painted his toenails with seasonal colours, green for Christmas, red for Valentine's Day, orange for Halloween. They stood shoulder-to-shoulder, naked, looking over the *duPont Registry*, a glossy lifestyle magazine for the affluent.

They tried on each other's $10,000 suits and shoes, admired each other's diamond studded rings and necklaces. It was an intense kind of camaraderie that to them felt completely natural, but was a little too close for my comfort.

I stood in the corner in baggy clothing or wrapped in an over-sized towel, dreading having to reveal my body on the walk to the showers. As I surveyed the room, I couldn't help chuckling to myself: And I'm the gay one. Hah!

Watching this thoroughly decent group of guys helped me understand why the presence of openly gay men who—as

Charles Barkley has said, are present in every single locker room—was so threatening. Coming out threatens to expose the homoerotic components of what they prefer to think of as simply male bonding.

And it generally is. It's not so much that there's a repressed homosexuality at play (except for a small minority), only that there's a tremendous fear that the behavior might be labelled as such. Or, as I heard the anti-gay epithets pour forth, that gay men in the locker room would somehow violate this sacred space by sexualizing it.

I always felt like saying, *Hey guys, let me reassure you from personal experience: Nothing could be farther from the truth.* I was plenty eager to desexualize the place, to live behind a carefully constructed façade of privacy. While I couldn't help notice a *few* attractive players during my NBA years, they always played for the *other* team. There's nothing like spending nine pressure-filled months with a bunch of sweaty, profane, ostensibly hetero guys to de-eroticize any environment.

And even if I did happen to find another player "hot," I wouldn't dream of checking him out, given the vulnerability of the social fabric of any team, not to mention the risk it would pose to my career. It just was not going to happen.

As Warren said of conditioning, it's as much about perception as reality. The problem lies in the confusion between the two.

●●●

By Christmas I'd hit a wall. After a fast start, my play deteriorated to the point where Fratello had rightly relegated me to long stretches on the bench. It didn't help that I spent some time on the DL with a strained rotator cuff.

In a mid-season assessment, the *Plain Dealer* put it bluntly: "Amaechi needs to work on his post-up moves, get into NBA shape, and develop better defensive footwork. If not, his NBA career will be short."

I couldn't disagree, but there were enough glimmers to give me hope. I played solidly against Detroit, where I blocked Grant Hill's shot twice. In Magic Johnson's second comeback attempt, when he played power forward, I remember nearly stopping in awe every time I saw him on the court but playing well anyway.

Against Chicago later in the season, I made a move to the basket while Michael Jordan approached from the weak side. Somehow I managed to get the ball around his outstretched wing and into the hoop. *I just beat Michael fucking Jordan,* I thought to my naïve, rookie self.

I'd done well enough to attract the interest of the British media, which treats basketball the way Americans view foreign policy, with a combination of apathy and disdain. In late January, the BBC sent a crew to follow me around for a few days. I was happy, not for egotistical reasons, but because the game needed all the attention it could get back home. Being one of the first Brits in the NBA is a little like being the tallest building in Cleveland. There's not a lot of competition. I just wished I'd been able to give the journalists some highlight reels to take home.

There was no mystery to why I had fallen off. I'd worked so hard over the summer and through training camp just to make the team that I had nothing left. Off the court I couldn't concentrate and slept all the time; on the court I struggled to keep up with the action.

It was all on me. I hadn't paced myself for the rigors of the pros—the stepped-up exertion of practices, the endless travel, the playing through injuries. The enormous stress of performing day in and day out, all under the looming possibility of the axe, exacerbated my exhaustion.

College ball was tough, but the season was less than half as long as the NBA schedule. Pro games started at 7 p.m., mostly for the benefit of prime time local television. Even if I didn't play much, people forget about the workout involved in stretching, warm-ups, and post-game workouts. I'd burn off several thousand calories by the time we finished at 10:00 or 10:30 at night.

Then we'd be whisked to an 11 p.m. flight for a two-to-four-hour journey. (Thank God Cleveland is in the middle of the map!) Getting rejuvenating sleep in the air is nearly impossible, especially since it's hard to stretch out my full frame.

We'd arrive in a strange town, get dumped off at a luxury hotel, and sleep for a few hours before it was time to make our way to yet another arena and start all over again.

What really wears you down is not the play or even the travel. It's the monotonous routine of it all. Endless hours spent waiting—for planes to board, for planes to land, for buses to snake through city traffic, for games to start.

Life, I soon discovered, is reduced to a succession of game plans, reviewing tape, stretching, warming up, trying to get focused on the game at hand. The joy that existed when I was playing with friends in England, before my hand injury, was gone. This was endless toil, and it never seemed to get easier.

Obviously, there were also plenty of rewards. We played well, going 47–35. Fratello had done a commendable job leading a scrappy bunch of overachievers into the playoffs, despite the fact that we were supposedly headed for lottery loserdom. Even though I wasn't a big contributor, averaging only 2.8 points in 28 games, it was a thrill to experience the excitement of the playoffs, especially since we took on the Knicks at Madison Square

Garden. (Thanks to the recent departure of circus animals, it was the worst smelling gym I'd ever stepped inside.)

I studied the great stars, Patrick Ewing and Charles Oakley, to see how they handled themselves, hoping I'd someday find myself with the opportunity to affect the outcome of a playoff game. Ewing always played hard, but I admired the humble aloofness about him, which gave the teams he captained a sense of confidence. I loved Oakley's attention to fundamentals and his hardscrabble approach, something I knew I'd have to perfect to make my mark on the game.

In my spare time I checked out Manhattan's sights and shopping districts, but never came back to the hotel loaded with gadgets and other bling as my wealthier teammates did. I tried to hide the embarrassing fact that I cherished the $300 road per diem, pocket change to the vets, knowing that it might not last much longer.

The Knicks swept us in three games. Nobody could blame me; I played all of two minutes. But even with my ass firmly planted on the bench, I wasn't complaining.

Just sitting in that storied place and taking it all in meant I'd arrived.

CHAPTER 14 ●●●] When in Athens

After the Cavs were eliminated in May of 1996, I flew to Manchester, where Joe Forber had asked me to appear at his Trafford Basketball Club, based in the suburb of Sale.

Joe started the club with a handful of teenagers in a concrete-floor gym. He trained one team a couple of nights a week, running the organization on a shoestring at various venues, from a 300-year-old Jesuit school, Stonyhurst College in Lancashire, to the University of Manchester facilities in the city center. It was a long way from American basketball.

Joe's mission was to provide an affordable space for young girls and boys to learn a game that was still exotic in England. Frankly,

Joe was more interested in the welfare of the kids than the game itself. For my part, I certainly had personal proof about the potential power of basketball, when properly harnessed, to sweep young people into an improbable journey of self-improvement.

The game had been good to me. Getting involved with Joe's club was another way I could give back by providing the same opportunity for the next generation, in the process making my career about something bigger and more meaningful than the possibility of fame and fortune.

Although we were starting on fumes and dreams, we soon envisioned a nationwide network of gyms, each with rooms for weights, cardio equipment, and classes, alongside several full courts, all staffed by the best full-time and volunteer coaches and athletic trainers around. These basketball centers, which would help fulfil my dream of one day working full-time with kids, became another motivator as I was launching my career.

Getting a network of centers off the ground would cost a small fortune, I knew, and at the very least I needed to come up with the seed money. With the sorry state of British basketball, government and corporate support would have to come later, after we'd proven ourselves.

It would require that holy grail of pro sports: A long-term NBA contract. The better I did on the court, the better I could do for these kids.

● ●●

After three rewarding weeks in Manchester, I flew back to Phoenix for another summer of gruelling workouts with my taskmaster, Warren.

On the flight, I met a married couple, Bob and Barb Filiere, and we struck up an immediate friendship. They were public school teachers, and we chatted about everything from basketball to raising kids. It turned out that one of their children had also attended St. John's in Toledo.

When I told them I'd be checking back into my dreary Phoenix efficiency, they offered me their guest bedroom. I ended up staying the summer and they became sort of surrogate parents, including me in family outings with their youngest child, Todd. It was a welcome dose of family comfort in a stressful time.

While I sweated in the desert, Bill fielded offers. As a one-year vet with playoff experience, my stock was rising. Cleveland wanted me back, but I knew there was a good possibility "the next big thing" in the draft might easily supplant me.

Clubs in Athens, Greece, and Barcelona, Spain, were among those vying for my services. They were offering close to a million *and* were willing to cover the taxes on the income, a standard practice in Europe—meaning I'd bring home close to double what I'd make from an American team paying a similar amount. The downside was that European owners were famous for reneging on contracts, failing to pay out the last several installments. For noncitizens, there was little recourse.

When I started hearing those kind of big figures from Europe, I was thrilled. It would be nice to be financially liquid again, as I'd spent my entire Cleveland salary on agent's fees, taxes, bills from as far back as college, and modest living expenses. And a few years of that kind of money would go a long way toward achieving Joe's dream (now also mine) of building our own basketball center.

At the same time, I was disappointed that there was not similar interest from the States. Despite the disappointing end to my rookie season, I believed I showed enough promise to warrant more substantial offers.

There was a factor more important than the money, however. Bill and I agreed that I could benefit from the seasoning. In Europe I'd play a lot, gaining invaluable court experience against some of the world's best players. In Cleveland I could be stuck behind Cage and a healthy Dougherty for another season.

The European leagues had gone from obscurity to international force in a couple of years. The great Croatian, Drazen Petrovic—who died in a car accident in 1993 while a member of the New Jersey Nets—served as the vanguard for an amazing influx of European talent to the NBA. The migration worked both ways; top NBA talent such as Byron Scott and Antonio Davis routinely played in Europe.

I chose Athens' Panathanaikos, partly because it was, well, Athens. I wasn't ready for a lonely seaside town in Spain, and I looked forward to checking out the sprawling modern metropolis built upon and around the ruins of ancient Greece. There were six first-division teams in the city alone, which had the benefit of cutting travel down substantially. We would still travel to Argentina and other countries, but we had the lightest travel schedule of almost any team.

The clincher was that the team was the reigning European champions and was coached by the great Bozidar Maljkovic, winner of four European titles. A short, stocky, balding man, he spoke a furious combination of Greek and French, with a smattering of English thrown in. He had won European championships in France and Greece, and he was hungry for more.

I was provided with a terraced hillside house in Kifissia, a northern suburb of Athens. The modern-style home had a spiral staircase, floor-to-ceiling windows, and groovy red easy chairs.

I was thrilled with such a fabulous place, close to the practice facility and right in the heart of the diplomatic and expatriate communities, where English was the common language.

By the time I'd reached St. John's, I'd started to comprehend the astronomical money ballplayers actually made, but it still always seemed unreal—what someone *else* might make. Now I was cashing six-figure checks. I wasn't giving it back, but in some ways I felt it wasn't entirely just. I was paid more for a few weeks of running up and down a basketball court than Mum had made treating desperately ill patients the entire time she worked in England.

Not at all confident of my pro future, I invested most of the money. There was one thing I wanted for sure: a house of my own. And not just any house. I needed a big house for a big man.

I decided that Phoenix would be my base, in part because I loved the stark beauty and dry heat of the desert, and in part because that's where Warren was. Call it Warren's House. If he hadn't been there for me in the beginning, I might not have had to means to build it. And if it wasn't located near him, there was a great chance I would never get to his workouts, especially given my well-known affinity for sweets and antipathy to voluntary exercise of any kind.

With the help of the Filieres, I found a development just outside Scottsdale, not far from Barb and Bob. The builder shipped me brick, tile, and carpet samples all the way to Athens. I used to get a kick out of opening the heavy overnight shipping packages and emptying out bags of bricks and tiles. I wondered what the postman thought I was up to.

After living the itinerant life, having my own home would give me stability, even if I was still globe- (or, even better, America) trotting. The house would have 15-foot ceilings, four spare bedrooms for my sisters and the friends I hoped to make, and a huge outdoor hot tub (right next to a fountain and pool) big enough for a seven-footer and featuring therapeutic jets.

It was also, at least in my dreams, the perfect party pad, and I imagined it overflowing with friends sipping margaritas, swimming, and chowing down on heaping barbeque in a big pit I would have installed in the backyard, the ultimate in al fresco dining.

I could count my friends on one hand, but there was no stopping a lonely boy from dreaming.

●●●

My decision to play in Athens looked even better when it turned out that John Salley, the former NBA star, had signed on as well. I was thrilled about the chance to learn from a low-post player I'd admired since I'd come to the States.

John had the kind of exuberant personality that quickly lifted me out of my dour moods. In the paint he was a warrior, and he dispensed tips to help me combat what had been exposed as my weakness in Cleveland: defense.

By getting too close to my man, I was giving away too much leverage for a defender with such a wide body. It was counter-intuitive: The closer you got, the harder it was to defend. "The only time your hips should touch another person is when you are having sex," Salley said with a laugh.

It was a memorable phrase, one that helped me improve and subtly exposed the hidden erotic pantomime of basketball, in which strapping men jockey for position under the hoop, body to body.

Despite his credentials, John was an unselfish player, and he had a knack for getting me the ball in the perfect spot. He could size up an opponent instantly, breaking down his weaknesses. That was a skill he shared with me, and it would give me confidence for years to come.

I learned a lot that season, not just from Salley but from the other guys as well. I entered the season thinking I knew how to set a pick—and I did. But there were nuances I was oblivious to, such as the optimal angle at which to set one. I learned a twist on what Michael Cage had been preaching, treating every play as a game within a game, where a single step could make or break the play.

Our relationship was not nearly so cordial with Maljkovic, the Serbian disciplinarian whose methods, we quickly learned, bordered on abusive. "Fuck your mother!" he'd scream in his native tongue.

During one practice, a player got hit in the balls, writhing in agony on the floor. When he sat up, Coach kicked him hard in the heel. "See? That will take the pain away," he said with a sadistic grin as he put boot into foot again.

He was the only one smiling. The rest of us looked on grimly at behavior that would never be allowed in any other civilized workplace.

On the first day of preseason, we went on a glorious run in the Alps. The sun was blazing, so I had on my polarized shades, not to look cool, but because my eyes water even on England's hazy days. "Nobody wears glasses," Maljkovic declared, snapping them off my head.

If he hadn't been the coach, I would have punched him right there on trail.

Salley got so fed up with such arrogance from a coach who clearly felt threatened by his own stars that he left after six weeks. John had more money than God, a great NBA career, including a title with Detroit, so there was little incentive to stay in an unhappy place.

I, on the other hand, had little choice but to endure.

This much I'll say for Bozidar: When it came to the game itself, he was first-rate. He could size up a team's strengths and weaknesses instantly, and strategize accordingly.

That was a critical skill in European play, because teams tended to be an odd mixture not only of styles but of nationalities. At the beginning of the season, the starting lineup included two Americans (Salley and Byron Dinkins), a Brit who played like an American (me), a German (Michael Koch), an Argentine (Hugo Sconochini), plus the league-mandated minimum of two native Greeks, both of whom were members of their national team. We were essentially a European All-Star team, with the national player of the year from every major basketball country represented.

By the end of the season, I could swear in nearly every European language.

Europe had not yet developed an American-style star system within its professional teams. Fame was derived more from your exploits for the national team. If talent was enough, we should have taken home the second consecutive championship that everyone had expected (and demanded). Every single player was a potent weapon. And we had the size to bully opponents into submission.

But basketball is the ultimate team sport. We won a lot of games, going 14–3 in league play. But that was usually against inferior teams, and against the best we faded, losing twice to our archrival, Olympiakos.

Like the U.S. Dream Team, knocked off by unheralded rivals at the 2004 Olympics, we rarely played better than five talented individuals who happened to wear the same forest-green uniform.

●••

Meanwhile, here I was in the cradle of homosexual civilization, but somehow, for the entire season, I barely managed to even glance at another man with lust in my heart. I didn't form a single crush, check out a single bar or club, frequent any of the hot spots.

When we were off, I'd head to my favorite hangout in Kifissia, down the street from my house, Windows Café, where I'd read, sip tea, and generally lounge the day away.

One evening I was there for dinner with one of my Greek-American teammates, Jon Korfas, when he looked across the room and said, lowering his voice, "That guy is the Elton John of Greece. He's famous."

The guy he pointed out did look a little on the flamboyant side. Not that there's anything wrong with that. Then Jon said something that shocked me.

"For awhile, I though you were one of *them*," he said, chuckling as he went back to feasting on his olives.

I wasn't sure how he came up with that notion, especially since he seemed to have no idea what *them* really meant. I could not have been less gay that year, though it was certainly not by choice.

I have an enormous capacity to *not* have sex, an ability that served me well early in my career, when hormones raged the hardest. There were distractions, of course, but generally not of the intensity my hyper-sexual counterparts on the team enjoyed (and sometimes suffered).

The fact was that my career would be damaged more if I'd picked the wrong partner, slept with the wrong person, and that was just one more reason to lead a chaste life. It was my first guaranteed contract, and I wasn't going to risk it on some random dalliance.

The wall-to-wall coverage in the half dozen or so tabloids in Greece made American journalism seem respectful by comparison. But my hetero teammates, screwing like bunnies, got off easy. They were expected to get laid, to be seen with the latest blond bombshell on their arm, to get caught in some strip club shoving drachmas into G-strings. Their sex lives were only news if they *didn't* have one.

●●•

Greeks believe basketball was handed down to them from Mount Olympus, rivaling soccer as their primary sport. If you asked them who invented basketball, they would claim ownership, despite considerable evidence to the contrary.

The rivalries run deep, creating a kind of tribal drama, a modern Iliad. The fans treat competition, city against city, team against team, green against yellow, with a ferocity that would shock even the most rabid American sports fan. The problem is that tribalism quickly descends into xenophobia.

American basketball is all about capitalism. Corporations buy up courtside seats and luxury boxes, which they fill up with suited executives and clients, the types who wouldn't dare make spectacles of themselves. Even those fans who foolishly launched themselves at players at Pacers games wouldn't stand a chance against the barmy armies of fans in European cities.

Greek basketball fans are decidedly more working class. The papers enflamed their fervor by scrutinizing players down to the short hairs. If I had 20 points, the headline would blare AMITZI (apparently my name in Greek) in bold letters. Or AMITZI TRE PUNTO when I'd nailed a clutch three pointer.

When I dared have an off night, there were other words beside my name the next morning that I normally only heard through clenched teeth.

When I was spotted sitting alone in a coffee shop, fans felt no compunction about plopping down at the table, as though as ticket owners they had bought the right. Their sense of entitlement was far greater than that of Americans, who, with notable exceptions, are content to idolize their sports stars from afar.

At game time, the court perimeter at the misnamed Peace and Freedom Stadium, a deep bowl arena with blood red seats, was lined with baton-wielding riot cops and whole sections up near the roof were kept empty to separate the warring factions. It was not exactly family-friendly fare.

The air stank of acrid smoke, mostly from freshly ignited road flares that fans lobbed at one another like hand grenades. During one game, a fan nailed Hugo Sconochini with a flare. His sweats, made of flammable nylon, soon burst into flames. Luckily, he had the presence of mind to stand up and rip them off, made possible by snaps designed to allow them to be quickly removed when entering a game.

Fans sharpened the edges of their drachmas, heated them with pocket lighters, and then hurled them down on the court. Poor Hugo took one off the head, blood spurting down his uniform and onto the floor.

There were plastic screens between the bench and the fans, the better to protect us from the spittle that showered opposing teams—or an underperforming home team. Not long into any game, a thick smog would settle over the court, the combination of chain smoking, flare fumes, and the small paper fires fans started to display their displeasure.

The young thugs loved the license to act out, probably more than they loved the game, and owners tolerated it because they were the only Greeks who shelled out for tickets and the cheap ouzo that you could buy in the stands.

Players put up with it mostly because of the money, and because it was an ideal proving ground for the NBA. It was all part of the deal. I understood that reality, but it was making me very unhappy.

To boost my spirits, about halfway into the season, I flew my sister Muriel and my Mum's best friend, Auntie Nelly, in for Christmas. When Muriel arrived, she was upset that I hadn't bothered with the traditional decorations, and she wanted a tree with all the trimmings.

So we headed down the narrow, winding road to a tree farm, where Muriel picked out her favorite. Since it was 8 p.m. on Christmas Eve when we arrived, there was no one around and we picked out a tree for free, jamming it into the back of the BMW 7 Series I drove since John Salley had left it behind. Muriel fit in the back underneath the tree with Auntie in front. We drove back up the hill, laughing hysterically as we frightened pedestrians with the overhanging pine branches along the way.

We ate Chinese takeout under the tree and watched British shows on satellite TV while marvelling at the glorious views of the city in the valley below.

●●●

Athens itself was like living in a time warp. A modern city struggled to crawl out from under the ancient ruins that were everywhere evident. The city exploded with sprawl and culture, the smog so thick I didn't even want to think about the particles I inhaled, especially when I was breathing heavily playing ball or working out.

I checked out the glorious remnants of the Parthenon and Erechtheum, which I'd only seen in college textbooks.

In my classics lessons at Penn State, I'd become transfixed by the myth of Chiron, the centaur who educated Hercules. (This is remarkable, because centaurs are known in mythology for being frivolous, reckless hedonists and Chiron was one of the few exceptions.) Wounded by a weapon that had been daubed in the Hydra's blood, he was said to be a great healer precisely because his own wound was forever open.

There was a psychological element to this myth that appealed to me, perhaps because with my unhappy childhood still very much a part of me, I saw myself as damaged goods. I took solace in the notion that those who survive damage gain insight and empathy, an attribute in which I took pride.

Then again, perhaps I was just flawed.

●●•

It crept up on me like a shadow in the afternoon. When I returned to my hillside home after a game or practice, I'd make myself dinner and pour myself a glass of rosé or white zinfandel, which quickly became a bottle or three, finishing the night with too much Bailey's Irish Cream. My sweet tooth was back with a vengeance, in a particularly vile form.

Now it was combined with a taste for alcohol, reminiscent of my underage drinking days with Peter. Except now, instead of a teenager goofing off with his friends, I was a grown man trying to establish himself in professional basketball.

The sweet elixirs went down so easily that I hardly noticed when the bottles were dry, usually because I'd have passed out, fully dressed, on the red couch in front of the *BBC World News.*

A few hours later, I'd be up early in the morning, refreshed, to shower, dress, head to practice, hang with my teammates. On my way home, I'd help out with the kids at The American School, known as TASIS, where I did my usual turn as a mentor, guest speaker, and all-around inspirational counsellor to troubled youth.

Since I maintained my work life, and I went about my responsibilities without thinking about drinking again until I got home the next night and poured myself a tall glass, I didn't think anything of it. Then the cycle of drinking and passing out would start again.

The emotional pain underlying my drinking was something no plan, no amount of discipline, could relieve. I was successful, I was contributing in a multitude of ways, but I was miserable, and not just because of the viciousness of the fans. There was no accounting for the ultimate variable, happiness. Naïvely, I believed that my achievement was supposed to translate automatically into happiness.

I can now say from hard experience, nothing is further from the truth. The cliché is true: You can't buy happiness.

My laser-like focus left little room for an emotional life, and now that I was on the verge of making it—achieving at least part of my goal—in the back of my mind there were nagging questions about how much more I'd have to give up in addition to how much I'd already lost. As a teenager with low self-esteem, basketball had given me a life, but it had also denied me one.

Despite the riches piling up in my savings account, I wondered for the first time whether I would not have been happier if I'd taken a road *more* traveled, become a child psychologist, a profession that would not only have given me more meaningful work but would have allowed me to assimilate into a gay community, perhaps in London or back home in Manchester. The idea of dating freely and having a sweet, playful posse of gay friends, something taken for granted by many urban guys my age, seemed a cruel phantom.

Instead, I had a growing bank account but few friends, no social life, and was utterly alone in a foreign land when I was away from the team. Not only did I not have a partner, I had absolutely no chance of finding one—not even the solace of a single night of love and affection.

I had no idea my drinking was out of control until Mike, one of my charges from TASIS, and his family came around for a visit. Mike brewed some tea as I chatted with his parents. When he opened the cupboard, it was filled exclusively with empty bottles. Nothing edible was anywhere in sight.

He was only a kid, but he knew something was wrong, shooting me knowing look as if to say, *What's this about?*

●●●

Sometimes an accident is an unhappy ballplayer's best friend. But sometimes an accident is just an accident. The trick is to tell the difference between the two.

After getting my first car at Penn State, I finally grasped the American love affair with the automobile. Not only are cars fantastic machines (there's nothing better than the roar of the engine as a car hugs a bend going 120), but they offer the ultimate freedom, the freedom of escape from your troubles.

America enjoys the best roads on earth. I could disappear from my regular life into a Zen-like state as I zipped across nearly empty roads through the valley and into the mountains. No pressure, no expectations, just communing with nature (okay, even while polluting it).

In Greece, I loved to cruise the mountain roads in my BMW, where you could enjoy magnificent panoramas. I loved navigating along the olive trees, the craggy heights on one side and the sheer drops on the other.

I carried the weight of the world. The fanaticism of the crowds had been traumatic, Bozidar was a tyrant, and I was as isolated as ever. None of these things would have been so bad if I had someone I could talk to. I chatted by phone with my sisters, sure, but locally I had few friends other than a couple of teammates. And then there was the *big* topic, which I had yet to broach with another human being.

Even at my worst, I never drove drunk. I can't even blame what happened on booze. In a flash I saw a curve ahead. For a split second, melodramatically, I wondered what it would be like to simply step on the accelerator and drive straight ahead, through the guardrail, careening off the cliff and down the mountainside.

Sure enough, perhaps distracted by my own fatalistic daydream, I reacted slowly to the bend in the road and ended up plunging into the low metal barrier.

On reflection, it's so *Thelma & Louise*. Yet when I look back on the accident, as I have every day since, I honestly can't say I did it on purpose. It was more a matter of fatal fantasy causing me to momentarily lose my concentration.

My subconscious was pulling the steering wheel and pushing the accelerator. Even in my darkest moments, I've never harbored suicidal thoughts. For all my flaws, I'm simply not the easy-way-out kind of person. I was hardly going to leave The Plan unfinished.

I felt a violent shaking, and then the car came to a sudden halt. When I lowered my arms, which had gone instinctively to my head, the front tires had stopped precipitously close to the cliff, the car held to the hillside by the ballasts. Looking down, I could see the lights of the city below, making me feel even more screwed up and irresponsible. It's one thing to end your own life; it's entirely another to risk the lives of others.

Once I realized I was stuck, I got out of the car and burst into laughter. It was like watching a scene in a movie, in which I'm the star doing something the audience knows is insane.

What an idiot! What a complete moron!

It was all so ridiculous, behaving like the bad Hollywood stereotype of a depressed person. Here I was in a para-suicide attempt, and I was hanging onto my life by the strength of a surprisingly solid Greek-built ballast.

Whatever the motive behind the crash, it was clearly a pretty good hint that I needed to figure out why I was so despondent, why I was drinking like a fish (okay, a *whale*), why I'd just crashed the team's cool $50,000 Beemer.

I assured myself I was no George Best, the soccer great who drank himself to death. But clearly, I could have blown everything I'd worked so hard to achieve.

I put the car in reverse and drove onto firm ground, then slowly coasted back down the mountainside to my house, leaving a dented railing in my wake, my life in the balance.

●••

The truth is, I did have one friend: an ancient tortoise who had taken up residence in the garden at the back of the house. He lived among the ferns and shrubs, and would show himself mostly when I brought him bits of salad. He was a grizzled old creature, not the prettiest tortoise I'd ever seen, but it was endearing to know he was there, an odd sign of wisdom and stability in a time when I lacked both.

Even though I have a bad tendency to name nearly everything in my path, (my current car, an awesome Audi W12, is known as Felicity), I never did name the fellow. Probably because tortoises, like manatees and whales, seem to defy trivial human labeling.

Once, after a blowing a home game, surviving the post-game pelting, and having a consoling dinner with the Koch family, I arrived back at my place. I parked and walked to the front door to a horrifying sight: the old boy's entrails were nailed to the front door. I knew immediately that the deed had been done by a deranged fan who had gotten hold of my address, supposedly a closely guarded secret.

I burst into tears. The poor tortoise had been there long before me, and though he was a bit slow-footed himself, he could hardly be blamed for my performance.

For God's sake, it's just a game, I said to myself. Even if we really are a bunch of lazy, losing bastards, to treat us like this is nothing short of psychotic.

This kind of behavior was all too common. Players had car windows smashed, the names of opposing teams scratched into the paint. After one of the last games I played, a few weeks after the tortoise was eviscerated, the owner threw his keys and big cup of Coke on the court, setting a perfect example.

Soon other heavy objects, such as batteries and the face plates of car stereos, landed not far from us. In a controlled panic, we raced to the locker room, changed, got into our cars, and drove out of the tunnel, only to find rows of thugs pelting us with rocks.

"We know where you live, bastard," they shouted. "You suck. You betrayed us."

I'm not sure they were even that articulate. But that was the gist of it.

I'd had enough of this depravity. I drove to my house, packed my bags, reserved a British Airways flight to London, and then, under the cover of night, headed to an airport hotel to await my flight.

I was following John Salley out the door a little earlier than I would have liked, but it wasn't safe to stay around for the last check—one that probably would never arrive anyway.

I felt my muscles relax as I walked toward the plane, and I started humming "Jerusalem," a habit I developed for trips back to England.

I fell fast asleep the instant the plane found air, awakening five hours later, when the wheels touched ground. I was home.

CHAPTER 15 ●●●] Home Sweet Home

The ancient Italian driver floored the Fiat up the windswept roads of the Apennine Mountains. Flashes of lightning illuminated the narrow passes.

It was like a scene from a cheesy horror film, and I half expected my chauffeur to turn around and look at me with a diabolical grin and yellow flashing eyes. My shouts of "SLOW DOWN" and "FOR THE LOVE OF GOD, STOP" fell on ears that didn't understand a word of English. I closed my eyes and hung on for dear life.

The trip back down in the light of day—at the end of a brutal training camp two weeks later, the Bee Gees' "How Deep Is Your

Love" blasting—made clear just how treacherous the drive had been, with sheer cliffs dropping away from the winding road. I took it to be a metaphor for the state of my career, not to mention my emotional life.

My 1997 tryout with the Portland Trail Blazers ended before camp had even started. I wish I could say I'd sprained an ankle hauling down a rebound or playing ferocious D. Instead, I slipped and broke my big toe heading to the hotel hot tub.

Bill's partner, Kenny Grant, was forced to work out another deal with another championship European team, this time Kinder Basketball Club in Bologna, which trained in the mountains. Hence the wild ride.

At that late date, I was lucky to have any gig. The money was nothing to complain about, but it still wasn't wealth I was after: My NBA dream seemed to be eluding my grasp.

It was a new team in a more tranquil place, but I hadn't resolved my sense of social isolation, my failure to open up about who I was. I was haunted by my inability to reconcile the romantic life I longed for with a career that all but prohibited it.

Italy has a thriving gay scene, despite the Catholic church's stranglehold. But I stayed away, still wary of the consequences of disclosure, spending most of my time by myself when I wasn't playing ball.

I moved into a cozy three-bedroom apartment in Bologna. The landlady spoke French, so I was able to communicate with her about the fuses that blew daily. Rather than fix the problem, she advised me to avoid using the stove, TV, and lights at the same time, so I kept the appliances in constant rotation.

To pass my downtime, I'd lounge in Piazza Maggiore, reading and sipping rich Italian coffee while listening to tourists chat. I loved checking out the old buildings with their vaulted ceilings, mosaics, and massive tapestries.

I enjoyed fresh *orecchiette* with tomato sauce, and a dessert that was better than sex (not that I was having any): chilled Mascarpone cheese with warm Nutella drizzles. It was a combination better even than the vaunted PB&J.

I couldn't complain about the club, one of the best groups of guys I'd ever played alongside. It amounted to another European All-Star team, featuring ex-Miami Heat star Predrag Danilovic, Hugo Sconochini of Argentina, Antoine Rigaudeau of France, and Racho Nesterovic of Slovenia (now in the NBA with the Raptors).

The Kinder coach, Hettori Messina, was a good man and a superb teacher. But he was the first of many coaches to insist that you can't play effectively unless you "love the game of basketball." I assured him I'd never loved the game but still played it pretty efficiently, a fact he was forced to acknowledge every time he wrote my name into the starting line-up, which was regularly.

I was willing to play through pain, physical and emotional, even in arenas in which spiteful fans pelt you with spittle and flares. But that certainly didn't mean I had to fall in love with the game itself. Lots of people who don't love their jobs are good at them. I was a professional, good at what I did, but nobody could make me love something I picked up more or less because I was tall and because I wanted a worldwide stage to prove myself.

The game chose me, after all.

In one way, Hettori was right. That year I was less enthusiastic than usual. I was, frankly, bitter about not getting another shot at the NBA, playing in basketball no-man's land. Even though I was still among the best players in the world, I believed I'd fallen far short of the goal sketched in The Plan. It was one thing to fail; quite another to never get the opportunity to fail or succeed.

But that year I had bigger problems than ball. I could count my friends on one hand, and I was still awful at socializing and meeting new people. Even back home in Manchester, I barely knew a soul beyond my sister, my friend Peter, and some of the guys from the national team with whom I played once in awhile. When I walked down the street, it was usually with music blasting in my ears so I didn't have to speak to anyone. Bearing down on 30, I still associated public appearance with adolescent public ridicule.

I remember running into a college professor back at Penn State who noticed that despite my celebrity, he often spotted me alone. He said something along the lines of, "You'll require a support group to get where you're going."

Now that sense of isolation—and lack of support—had become intolerable. Again and again, I asked myself the same question: Why am I this person who plays basketball when basketball not only fails to make me happy but makes me downright miserable?

I needed someone, anyone to talk to. Plenty of guys I'd played with suffered personal problems from time to time. It was only natural. But they had girlfriends, wives, or at least parents to turn to. Even team officials could listen to their problems and point them toward help.

That wasn't an option for me. And despite being close to my sisters, just thinking about disclosing my secret always felt like I was unloading an unfair burden on them. I'd never uttered a word about it to Mum, although Muriel said Mum once asked her if I might be gay. Muriel didn't know enough to give her an answer, but when she asked if it would matter, Mum shrugged and said "no."

I'd been coming home to an empty apartment for far too long.

As I thought through the limited options, my mind rested on Sandy Meyer. Sandy had been the academic advisor to varsity athletes back at Penn State. When Mum died, she'd been there for me, becoming a surrogate maternal figure. I'd spent a lot of time with her over my college career, having dinner at her house, watching movies, just hanging out.

I wrote Sandy an e-mail telling her what was on my mind without actually ever declaring, "I'm gay." She wrote back immediately, and I eventually got her on the phone.

I finally worked up the courage to use my name and *gay* in the same sentence. I sobbed into the receiver. Two hours later, I was still sobbing. I wasn't crying because of the truth. That part felt good. I was crying at the sense of relief, the years wasted on repression, the tyranny of my own expectations, my internal confusion, the ugliness of bigotry. I mourned the emotional terrain that had been my life since I picked up a basketball as a late teen.

Sandy wasn't fazed. A female friend and volleyball player, she explained, had once wondered aloud why I had not "made a move on her," so she put two and two together.

Mostly, Sandy just listened, comforted, and assured me that everything would be all right.

●••

More than anything, I wanted to walk away for good. Go home and relax, lead an ordinary workaday existence. Part of me knew that would be a huge mistake, a decade of dedication wasted. But I couldn't work up the energy to care. I needed out, no matter what. Human beings can only tolerate so much misery before they rebel. And that was what I was determined to do.

When the club, predictably, stopped paying me halfway into the season, I had the perfect pretext for departing. Kenny gave management an ultimatum: "Pay up or Amaechi is leaving." I was one of the best players on the team, so it was no idle threat. When checks were not forthcoming, I called Bill and Kenny and calmly informed them I was quitting.

Panicked at the thought of the rash decision I was about to make and the millions I was potentially leaving on the table, Kenny got on the next flight to Bologna.

The problem was that neither Kenny nor Bill knew the whole story, and I wasn't ready to fill them in on the details. I mean, I could barely tell Sandy. How was I going to tell these guys who were making their living in the NBA, sports guys deeply embedded in the industry? I had no reason to believe these decent men would have been anything but completely supportive. But I was too scared to think rationally.

I took Kenny to dinner at my favorite place near the piazza, where we talked about my career over fresh pasta and beef. He understood that I was unhappy, appreciated the fact that I was not your average athlete, but insisted anyway that it was way too early to throw in the towel. He argued that I was still in my prime, had an NBA future "written all over me," and that they could find me another team.

I appreciated the trouble Kenny had taken to provide a boost. Of course, he and Bill were right. It was no time to quit; I wasn't a quitter. The Plan would not allow it. It would have been a disgrace to Mum's memory and all the efforts of the generous people who'd helped me get this far.

The problem was that in my current emotional state, I couldn't keep playing.

We settled on a compromise. I would return to Manchester and they would find me a nearby British team.

Then I would get a life.

●••

It was good to be home, and my mood lightened with every day I spent on English soil. I stayed with Muriel in Stockport, where I celebrated Christmas 1998 and New Year's in my hometown for the first time in a decade.

Shortly thereafter, I joined the Sheffield Sharks, the previous year's English Cup winners, and the team leased me an apartment. I commuted back and forth between home and Sheffield over the mountain range that separated them in the cheap Volvo the team provided.

I drove like a man possessed, bombing over the "snake pass" with its hairpin turns at 50 miles an hour, having absorbed none of the reckless driving lessons of Greece and Italy. This time I drove because I had somewhere to go, not just to escape.

I was equally aggressive on the court, and it showed. I was pretty dominant. No, I take that back. I was *simply* dominant. In the championship game, which we won, I scored 40 points. The standard of play was shit, but my confidence was returning in waves.

The club was a massive step down from European ball, but I stayed in shape while having a chance to decompress in the less competitive environment.

The British Basketball League had refused to let me join Manchester, my local team, saying it would give them an "unfair advantage," which I'd always thought was the point of bringing in good players, especially well-known, home-grown ones.

Sharks general manager Yuri Matischen told me before I signed that Sheffield would be the "white horse" I could ride on to "change English basketball" for the better. White elephant was more like it.

Nearly a decade later, the league is still the poor stepchild of European basketball, refusing to make the most basic effort to raise the level of play and fan support.

As I did most summers, I worked out with and played for the English national team. I was only 28, but I'd always been considered the mentor, the wise older guy, mostly because I'd had a career in the NBA—even though at that point it had only been one season. In a country with a population of 60 million, that status should have meant a lot—except for the fact that very few of those 60 million gave a damn about basketball.

It was easy to see why. When we went abroad for tournaments, we were woefully under-prepared and under-funded. A motley crew of ballplayers, we stayed in run-down accommodations after suffering grueling travel conditions just to get there. It was little wonder we couldn't compete.

Even by these standards, our Ukrainian adventure was gruesome. It was a dark time in the Eastern Bloc nation, riot police lining the streets. We were not allowed to leave our shabby hotel in Kyvic for fear that we'd be shaken down by the cops. If the assistant coach had not had the foresight to bring along a case of Pot Noodles (just add boiling water!), I swear we would have gone hungry.

One of our players was arrested for jaywalking, handcuffed, and placed in the back of a police van. Our coach, Laszlo Nemeth, intervened, and the player was released to his custody. As a native of Hungary, Laszlo knew his way around the cultures of the Eastern Bloc. A very modest bribe did the trick.

Laszlo is one of the few highlights in the dim history of British ball, a world-caliber coach who made a valiant effort to revive the moribund state of our game. He was always saying that we had the potential to be an international force. He would know, having coached everywhere from Italy to Saudi Arabia.

He'd spent his own money making sure the trip came off.

On another trip, to Bucharest, Laszlo took us on a tour of the city's ancient Turkish baths. Naturally, I'm not one for nakedness, and the towels provided made fig leaves look prim, so I fetched a proper oversized one. Then I joined my teammates and a host of locals for a hot mineral bath, followed by a vigorous massage by two men who beat the hell out of my body with scouring pads. (I've never liked the butterfly kisses most people call a massage.) Then they grunted, hosed us down with warm water, and sent us out into another dip in the mineral water.

When he wasn't treating us to a spa experience, Laszlo was drilling us relentlessly in the fundamentals. He was a technician who, like Joe Forber, knew how to break the game down into component parts.

I was one of the most experienced players on the team, but my late start meant I still had the capacity and the desire to know more, to improve. Laszlo had a book of technical tricks that were more about team play than individual. Among other things, he taught me how to make my team look good when I was constrained by double teams. The blues were lifting, and

I was starting to hope that I could once again turn some of that knowledge into another shot at the NBA.

Because there was no place to play at home, the best British players had fanned out across the globe, and Laszlo corralled them all on the national team for this brief period. We at least had a fighting chance.

But even Laszlo got fed up. That was his last season in Britain.

CHAPTER 16 ●●●] Beautiful Things

One of the few advantages of playing in Britain was that since the sports pages barely covered basketball, we were not driven to distraction about our private lives by the British tabloids, which make the *National Enquirer* look like *The New Yorker*. That provided me the space I needed to explore, a space that would also have been difficult to secure in big American cities, where players' hijinks are covered like a blanket.

While playing for the Sharks, I began to make tentative forays into Manchester and Sheffield gay life. For years, the best I could do was walk or drive by a gay establishment, and now I was eager to actually cross the threshold of one. Or seven.

It was high time see whether there was any way that kind of a life dovetailed with the macho, itinerant life of the pro ballplayer.

Thanks to the Internet, it was now much easier to explore dating anonymously than it had been just a few years earlier. One late night, I chatted online with a guy for awhile and we agreed to meet.

David seemed a nice enough fellow, so I told him to look for "the tall guy" at an Italian restaurant in Sheffield. I hadn't been this nervous since my date with Amber way back in high school, when I also sweated through my shirt.

I'm still not even sure whether he was attractive. When the waiter came, all I could do was to point at something on the menu (which turned out to be penne arrabiatta, the spiciest dish there, contributing to the beads of perspiration dripping down my body). David, however, wasn't anxious at all, having done this kind of thing many times before. I chatted awkwardly through dinner, and then we headed back to my place. We sat on the couch with a pillow between us watching *Beautiful Thing*, a gorgeous movie about love between two British boys living in housing projects.

It was the perfect date movie, but the working-class teens on the screen, for all their struggles, were far more advanced than me. For once there was a happy ending to a story about same-sex love. It gave me hope for the future.

The present, however, was another thing. After the credits rolled, I ushered David out of the door and went to bed—alone. I did not see him again.

He was lovely, but I didn't even ask for a kiss.

Typical.

● ● ●

On New Year's Eve, Muriel informed me she had plans with friends to ring in the New Year at Cruz 101, a gay club in Manchester. Muriel is not gay, but her friends were an eclectic mix of sexual orientations, male and female, and they all adored going out to what was at the time the hottest club in the city.

"Cruz is a *gay* bar," she warned me. "So if you want to come along, behave. Be nice to *them.*"

I chuckled to myself.

I'd never given her reason to think I was hostile to gay people or to any another minority group. But she knew enough gay men to know how poorly they are often treated by the über-macho, many of whom are ballplayers.

Given my anti-social tendencies, she must have been surprised at my enthusiasm.

It wasn't clear to me whether I was going as straight, gay, or asexual. Inside I was gay. To the outside world I was not. The reality was that I'd spent the last several years without any erotic or romantic attachments at all.

The answer to my nervous confusion was easy: I walked right up to the bar, started ordering stiff drinks, and got hammered.

The club was heaving with energy—the pulse of Michael Jackson and '70s R&B. The dance floor was crowded with sculpted, shirt-less male bodies. Strobe lights illuminated cigarette smoke that wafted to the rafters. It was the kind of night where anything can happen and usually does. Some guy squeezed my ass (and *not* a gentle ballplayer's pat). When I turned around, he winked, which I quite liked.

Another guy came up and whispered in my ear, "I know who you are. It's great to see someone like you come into a place like *this.*"

For a moment I was horrified, imagining I'd blown ten years of meticulous cover. But then I smiled at the compliment, that my presence mattered, that perhaps basketball would give me a chance one day to make a difference to these brave guys as well.

Some time later, I was washing my hands in the men's room when a cute guy leaned in for a smooch. I eagerly leaned down to reciprocate when the doorman, a friend of Muriel's, walked out of a toilet stall.

Smiling, he joked, "I'm gonna tell your sister!"

I figured I should do the job myself. I told Muriel I'd written her a note. I still couldn't bring myself to say the word, so I'd scribbled, "I'm not as straight as you might have thought."

When I handed it to her, I told her she was not to read it until I'd left. It was an unfair request, but she was good enough to honor it.

"I always assumed you were asexual," she said the next time she saw me. I could understand how she had gotten that impression. I hadn't given her a clue in either direction, so it was the only logical conclusion.

Then she told me she loved me.

I used the same technique with my old friend Peter.

After a night of drinking at his place, I got up early and cracked open the door to his bedroom. He was passed out on his bed, breathing heavily. I crept in quietly and left another "not-as-straight-as-you-might-have-thought" note on his chest.

A few hours later I got a phone call.

"John, I knew that when you were 16," Peter said. "It doesn't matter to me at all. You are my friend no matter what."

Big sigh of relief.

"But John," he continued with a laugh. "Just one thing: No more notes!"

I was mock indignant. All I could think was, *He knew when I was that young? Why was I the last to know?*

New Year's Eve was so much fun that we made a habit of going out. It was the first time since high school that I'd lived a relatively normal life, socializing with a growing group of friends while I was playing—and playing exceptionally well, in fact—for the Sharks.

At first I was too nervous to walk along Canal Street, the center of the gay neighborhood. But it wasn't long before my bar became Via Fossa, where I was as regular as Norm at Cheers.

To my shock, I became a relentless flirt. I even managed a few relaxed dates. It was a dating crash course. Like basketball, it took me awhile to learn the rules of the game. Starved for attention and never having done this before, I said yes to every invitation. *Okay, you find me attractive, let's go,* was my general approach.

It took me back to those days at Penn State, groping some guy in the upstairs bathroom, a fevered wham-bam, thank you, man. Except now I was actually getting to know these guys. I'd been celibate since college, and it didn't feel right to go back to anonymous encounters again. I needed something more, something that would have the warmth of romance *and* friendship.

It was during another Cruz 101 outing that I said hello to an attractive guy with a nice smile who was standing near me. I was in my customary place, standing at the bar watching the dancing while sipping my favorite, Gin and Slim lime tonic. I loved the way the drink glowed under the ultraviolet light.

His name was Darren. We chatted for awhile, and then went our own ways. I was too drunk even to remember that I'd given him my phone number. So I was pleasantly surprised when, a few days later, he called. We saw each other steadily, my first experience with what ordinary 20-somethings know as dating.

He was kind, strong, no-nonsense. He was a nurse, and had the nurturing aspect to his personality of many in the medical profession. He was more amused than anything at my line of work, since basketball carried no weight in England. But he did think I was lucky not to have what he thought of as a "real" job.

It wasn't even the sex that I enjoyed the most. Contrary to the demeaning rhetoric of "gays as sex fiends," my fondest memory of our time together was going over to his house and being so exhausted that I fell asleep, my head in his lap in front of the fire that warmed the house on chilly nights.

It dawned on me that I'd finally found a safe place in the world when one evening, as I was ordering a drink before Darren's arrival, the bartender asked me where my boyfriend was. I'd spent all this time avoiding these places, and suddenly it felt liberating that someone assumed I was gay. And that it was no big deal at all, just another aspect of everyday life.

●●•

They say all good things must come to an end. For a ballplayer without a job, all things come to an *early* end.

At the end of the Sharks' season that spring, I said goodbye to Muriel and Darren and flew to Arizona for more workouts with Warren. I told Bill I was ready for one last NBA shot, and that required getting into the best shape of my life.

As for Darren, I would continue to see him from time to time, but we both knew that if I ended up back in the States, our relationship would draw to a close. The Manchester-Phoenix commute made a mockery of the term "long-distance relationship," and frankly, I still wasn't sure I was ready to be seen in public with a male partner. Gay friends, to be sure, but the whole partner thing felt a road too far. Darren, busy in his own career, agreed. Our split was largely amicable, and we remain friends to this day.

To some degree, I knew I was heading right back into the closet I'd toiled long and hard to find my way out of. But I also vowed that if I made it back to the NBA, I'd do whatever I could to carve out a safe little gay niche for myself. And that after my career ended, I could obliterate the closet door in a big way.

In the meantime, I knew, sacrifice was an unfortunate but critical part of The Plan.

Thanks to my ability to stick to Warren's rigorous routine, I got into my best shape ever. (I know I said that every year, but this time it was true!) I didn't quite attain that elusive beach body some of the other guys boasted, but I came pretty close.

More important, I felt great. Born again, in fact. I knew who I was. And I knew what I wanted. I could get there from here.

Bill landed me a tryout with the Toronto Raptors. In the days before Vince Carter, this was a team of relative unknowns. And for a reason: they sucked. Yes, there were talented guys like Damon Stoudamire, Marcus Camby, and Tracy McGrady, but their big man was the injury-prone Sharone Wright.

And what was not to like about Toronto, one of the most beautiful and socially progressive cities in the world? I had a café in the gay 'hood all picked out.

We figured this was my best shot since Cleveland. I'd established myself as one of the top players in all of Europe, two years running, but there was another continent to conquer.

During my tryout, I blew everyone away in an endurance drill in which you run the length of the court in ever-decreasing amounts of time. You start out walking and end up in a flat-out sprint, a combination of endurance and speed that'll leave even the best-conditioned athletes crumpled on the floor, gasping.

At the end of the drill, I was the last man standing.

Athletic trainers have a unique vantage. They may not know X's and O's, but they can tell the whiners from the winners, the distracted from the disciplined. After checking out my conditioning and work ethic, they declared, practically in unison, "You *must* play here."

Trainers are not coaches, however, and while I left camp with encouraging words from the coaching staff, there was also a sense of "Don't call us."

I showed enough to warrant another tryout with the team, but then came the labor strife. The owners locked out the players, and nobody, from Michael Jordan to a nomad like me, was getting paid—brutal for guys on the bubble for whom a few months can make or break a career. I prayed for the standoff to end quickly so I could hook up with another team, but to no avail.

Bill lined up another big-bucks deal to play for Limoges in the French basketball league about halfway into the European season. While it wasn't the NBA, I was a Chunnel ride from home, so I'd even be able to meet Darren in Paris or London once in awhile.

I was given a fabulous apartment overlooking the main square, perhaps the most charming place I'd ever lived. One of my fondest memories is of being awakened early in the morning by the sound of children racing across the square to school.

I also remember the ancient wooden floors that creaked no matter how lightly you trod. I remember trying to order Chinese food in French from the restaurant next door—not an easy task. I remember the X-rated cable TV channel. God, the French have a talent for gay porn.

On the court, my play remained at a high level. It was a tremendous feeling, knowing for a fact that I was the best player in the house. My superior stamina and conditioning gave me a big advantage, especially over the French players who were not known for their hard workouts.

My midrange jumper had improved to the point where I had the confidence to drill it whenever I had a good look. And defenders soon realized they couldn't overplay me, because my inside game was actually my strength. It seemed that season I was always on the line, an easy way to pad your stats and give your team an advantage.

The fans were fantastic, loyal, and knowledgeable, but also respectful, as opposed to those in a more eastern part of the world that will go unnamed. They took to me immediately, and I became sort of a mini-legend in that rather sedate part of the country.

To my shock, Limoges had brought in my old nemesis Bozidar Maljkovic as an assistant coach. I half expected John Salley to show up next. Whether it was the change in scenery or the passage of time or an increase in my own tolerance level, we got along famously, and we spent some time catching up and sizing up the young players on the team.

He called the young French players "petit" regardless of their size, and the young Russian player on the team "mali," "little one" in Russian. It was an amusing endearment because it was not a word one generally associated with basketball players.

CHAPTER 17 ●●●] # Heart and Hustle

In 1999, coming off three brutal European seasons and four teams, I was about to turn 29—relatively old by athletic standards. I was running out of chances.

The good news was that NBA scouts had come back with good reports on my European play. I'd addressed the weaknesses in defense and rebounding that had sent me overseas in the first place. I was convinced I was strong enough to avoid a repeat of my Cleveland collapse. I knew how to pace myself. I hadn't even laid eyes on a Twinkie in three years.

Bill convinced the Orlando Magic to make room for me at a pre-summer league for non-roster invitees, no-hopers, also-rans, cast-offs, washed-up veterans, and late draft picks. I fit right in.

He believed it was a good fit. The Magic still lacked a star center, opening the door for someone like me. Shaq had ditched Orlando years earlier for the biggest contract in NBA history and the Hollywood lifestyle, and I would be more than happy to cover a small chunk of the gaping hole in the paint he'd left behind.

I played well enough to earn an invitation to play for the team's entrant in an Atlanta summer league, a showcase for up-and-coming talent as well as veterans, such as Steve Nash, looking to stay in shape and hone their game.

I kicked ass.

European ball had served me well. What that game lacks in speed, it makes up for in fundamentals. It's not just run-and-gun. Take Arvydas Sabonis, the seven-foot-three Lithuanian who learned the game in Europe and became the Trail Blazers' star center. His mechanics, smarts, and court awareness made up for his lack of leaping ability and quickness. (By comparison, Arvydas made me look light-footed.) In a summer league where guys rely on athleticism rather than technique, I stood out.

When it came time for training camp, Orlando and Phoenix extended invitations. I would have preferred to stay close to home—I'd fantasized about playing in Phoenix and then driving home to my own hot tub and bedroom—but Orlando offered me $20,000 guaranteed, which was twice what Phoenix was willing to fork over. I had turned down more than $1 million to play in Europe. The extra cash gave me a hint about Orlando's willingness to provide an honest opportunity.

Even on the fringes, NBA money is so plentiful that it's easy to get caught up in the game. Playing back in the States again, there were constant reminders of how lucky I really was, and how easy it is to lose perspective. After night games, a fleet of shiny Porsches, Benzes, and SUVs—probably a million dollars worth of steel—pulled out from the players' parking lot into the dimly-lit streets of downtown Orlando.

The moment my own Chevy Tahoe passed the last security gate and the screaming crowd of super-fans (if we'd had a good game), we were confronted by a different world. The sidewalks were cluttered with homeless men and women, sleeping under awnings, on coats and cardboard. These people, some quite young, would have considered our rides luxury homes, except that they were designed not just to be comfortable but to keep the outside world away, with the hushed, serene interior, security systems, and armored exteriors.

Most of the players, accustomed to inner city poverty (and sometimes produced by it), barely gave these people a second glance. It never ceases to amaze me how in America, the land of extremes, the richest of the rich and the poorest of the poor exist so closely without ever combusting.

●●•

Training camp for a non-roster invitee is surreal, another basketball no-man's land. I didn't know up from down, especially since I was in the middle of a strange new city where I didn't know a soul. Even in the autumn, the humidity made scorching Scottsdale seem mild.

Fifteen men vied for 13 spots. With the absence of marquee players, there was plenty of opportunity. From what Bill and I surmised, for the final big-man roster spot I was up against two vets, Armon Gillian and Terry Davis.

Despite the competition, they graciously offered guidance. During one practice, Armon demonstrated one of his patented low-post moves that, he insisted, "Will keep you in this league for a long time," perhaps signaling that he understood more about the personnel situation than I did.

In the dog-eat-dog world of the pros, it's uplifting when vets mentor new players, especially when it's not necessarily in their own interest. In my first year with Cleveland, players gave me everything from sports drinks to jackets and shoes. Some of which they got for free from sponsors, but it still made me feel welcome.

Orlando's new head coach, Doc Rivers, demonstrated he meant business, launching our first practice at midnight, demanding six 17's (sprints the entire width of the court in less than 50 seconds with one minute of rest in between). To this day it amazes me that I could pull this off, because I now lose my breath climbing the stairs to my apartment. I was among the best-conditioned big men, but the super-human Bo Outlaw blew the rest of us away. Bo could run the court in four strides and turn on a dime.

Doc's disciplined approach gave me hope that he was looking for guys like me—no-nonsense, hard-working—the opposite of the stereotype of the arrogant, spoiled ballplayer. I knew I didn't have the luxury of preseason nonchalance, unlike players with guaranteed contracts. As in my first year in Cleveland, I kept my head down, playing hard and smart even when my shooting was cold as ice.

I got the usual praise from the trainers, who appreciated my dedication to the workout routine, even when it included the despised weight room. In fact, the trainers were concerned that

I was working too hard, losing too much weight—surely the only time I've had *that* problem.

After a summer of dominance, I proceeded to play my worst. Shots clanged off rims, guys blew past me for easy dunks. Balls went off my fingers and out of bounds. I seemed to have left my confidence back in France.

I barely heard a word from coaches, who avoided providing even the slightest indication of where I stood. My fellow players, most of whom were too busy trying to make their own mark to offer encouragement, were similarly mum. I figured out I'd made the team when a front-office secretary casually directed me to "go ahead and rent an apartment."

Despite my wretched performance, Doc told me later he was confident that the intensity of my desire was a fit for the scrappy brand of team he was building. I think he saw my struggles for what they were: the pressure of getting back on an NBA roster after three years of trying. He was rolling the dice. It meant that Gilliam and Davis were cut loose, with the team eating their multi-million-dollar contracts.

I was proud to have overcome a bigger obstacle: the constant predictions of my demise. The preseason papers were full of articles speculating about when I would be cut and the "real" team pulled together. I made mental notes of the digs, to better gloat when my time came.

One of the most difficult tasks for any player is finding ways to avoid being consumed by critics, worry, and self-doubt. The media loves a flop more than a hit, and it is easy to get trapped inside the day-to-day prognostications of beat reporters. They tend to focus on your pitfalls, rather than your potential—by definition unseen and unproven. It is imperative to remain focused on the potential, so I made a habit of visualizing my forte, from a soft shooting touch to low-post moves.

I celebrated making the team by going to bed early. My struggle, I knew, had only just begun.

● ● ●

Great teams are their own marketing slogan. But every season, second-rate franchises come up with a PR spin intended to inspire fans in a way the players can't. Inevitably, as the team languishes, the spin becomes a running joke.

That year we were dubbed HEART & HUSTLE, and billboards blaring it went up across town. The sentiment was based on the roster, which was filled with overachieving team-oriented players. There was hardly a star among us. The posters didn't include our faces because the marketing was aimed at inspiring ticket buying, not, *Who the hell is that?*

Chucky Atkins and I came from Europe. Bo Outlaw and Darrell Armstrong were supposed to be on the downside of their careers. Other teams had cast adrift Pat Garrity, Ben Wallace, and Ron Mercer. Michael Doleac was unproven. Our lone standout, Penny Hardaway, had been dealt to Phoenix before the season. Four of our starters hadn't even been drafted.

We were in "rebuilding" mode. In other words, management had created an inexpensive roster of cast-offs likely to fail badly enough to bring a high lottery pick, which would supposedly transform the franchise. We were expendable, the NBA version of the Bad News Bears. Our role was to be lovable losers, to entertain for a year, and then disappear.

No one believed the hype. Shaq's departure had plunged the city, already afflicted with a sports inferiority complex, into a basketball tailspin. The roster looked scarily like the expansion team it had been not that long ago. It seemed every opponent in the Eastern conference was more talented, replete with stars with fat contracts and a bevy of solid role guys.

Boston had Paul Pierce, the Sixers Allen Iverson, the Knicks Allan Houston *and* Latrell Sprewell, Indiana the slick Reggie Miller. We were hoping to stay competitive, avoid embarrassing blowouts, and sort out whether anyone was worthy of keeping around for the future.

Sure enough, it got ugly quickly. We lost seven in a row early on.

Sometimes you can predict the future of a team as much by the way it loses as the way it wins. And the good thing was that guys never moped, complained, or gave up. And with every setback, Doc cracked the whip, so we showed up earlier and stayed later.

Then something funny happened: We started to win. And not just against lousy teams. We took down the three best teams in the East: the Heat, the Pacers, and the Knicks. The hard work paid off, L's became W's. Even defeats were hard fought. Teams complained bitterly that we were a bitch to play against because we contested every pass, every shot, and basically made opponents battle for every inch of court.

Teams loved to say we "surprised" them. We smiled when we heard that pathetic excuse. In the NBA, scouting is executed to perfection. You literally know how many dribbles a point guard will take before he passes, what his favorite move is, and the percentage of free throws he hits in the fourth quarter. I once caught a glimpse of my Phoenix scouting report. It noted that I drove left 73 percent of the time.

What our opponents actually meant is that they took us for granted. Talented teams often operate under the illusion of superiority on paper. In reality, it's not enough to *be* better; you actually have to play better.

While we lost some games because we were outclassed, some because we were exhausted, and a couple due to rookie mistakes, we never lost because we didn't show up. There is a baseline of talent below which no amount of preparation can compensate. We were above that line. Just barely, but enough to put the intangibles into play.

When it became clear that we were actually better than in the past—even without the incomparable Shaq—the city lavished us with love.

Fans, of course, can be fickle. When we went through rough patches on the road, blowing three or four games in a row, we dreaded returning home. But they stayed right there with us. They could see that we left blood on the floor, sometimes quite literally, every night.

The victories piled up, and the team inched past .500 and into contention. Nine consecutive wins at the end of the year put us within shouting distance of a playoff berth.

After sitting out the first few games, I edged up to about ten minutes per game—just enough to show my stuff and win Doc's confidence. My shooting touch had returned, and I was becoming the go-to guy in the limited court time I saw.

I joked with Monty Williams that I'd get Doc a point for every minute I played, making it impossible for him to sit me—the boast of every guy who is productive in limited minutes. Spread out over a 60-minute game, I'd have been putting up huge numbers.

Bo Outlaw, Ben Wallace, and I formed a closeknit front court that fed off one another's work ethic and enthusiasm. We valued teamwork over individual glory, and our skills were complementary. I was the scorer; Ben the rebounder, enforcer, and defender;

Bo the X-factor who would surprise teams with his stamina, speed, and tenacity.

I'd never played on a team in which jealousy was so completely absent. The "my turn" syndrome, in which players resent it when one guy get too many touches, just didn't exist. In fact, we would ride a guy for as long as he was hot. The backup players, who would be rotting at the end of the bench on more talented teams, became known as the Magnificent Seven for our contributions. We ran opposing starters into the ground by constantly rotating fresh bodies onto the court.

Like any true team, we complemented one another. Ben, for instance, lacked an outside shot. But he was a tenacious defender who corralled lose balls like a kid hoarding Halloween candy. He had one simple rule: Once a rebound is in the air, don't fight him for it. Which was fine with me. As the ground-bound one, I was hardly going to mess with his aerial superiority.

Then there was Doc. Only a few years removed from his days as a star point guard, he was young enough to relate to his players and accomplished enough to command respect. After I was getting hammered early in the year without foul calls, Doc complained in the press that refs were "giving Amaechi no respect." He earned a fine for his outburst. But, having been put on notice, the zebras started giving me more calls—another factor in my success.

He also appreciated that for me, basketball was only one part of my life. He knew that I listened to Mozart and wrote bad poetry. That I hung out at cafés and art galleries and volunteered with kids. That I didn't go out much at night because I had no friends outside of basketball.

In the game plan of life, Doc knew that basketball was a means to an end. None of that bothered him. In fact, he'd often check out my web site and comment on my latest verse or a posting blasting the National Rifle Association.

●●●

My play really clicked before the All-Star game in January. Doc was easing me into the rotation, and the more I played, the better I got. I ran the break well, and I'd pick up six points just by filling the lanes. I pulled centers away from the basket and hit jumpers over them. In the post, I'd finesse my way around their bigger bodies, never trying to go over them. My hard-earned skills were finally on full display.

When we went to our set offense, Darrell would get me the ball on the "right block that Meech owns," as one of the assistants told me. No one could complain. I was making the most of my chances, partly by exploiting my ambidexterity to finish—one of the many things Tim Duncan does so well. It meant defenders had no way of predicting which way I would go, leaving me with many easy put-backs.

But my greatest strength was my awareness of what I *couldn't* do. I knew better than to try to beat an opponent at what he does best. A lot of big men can't resist the temptation to take the battle directly to Shaq or Duncan. The time you dunked on the best makes a great story to tell your grandkids. But most of the time such a challenge ends in failure. Undersized for a center, I had no illusions of being stronger than Shaq, Alonzo Mourning, or Patrick Ewing, the best big men of my era.

In my first game in L.A. with Orlando, I faced the ultimate test. It was unnerving to share the sidelines with Hollywood celebrities clamoring for attention from the Lakers' stars while

second half, slowing me to five points in a loss, but I'd clearly earned my due. I was simply too quick for most centers in the league, man to man.

That sounds arrogant, I know, but the best defenders in the world couldn't find a solution. Against Hakeem Olajuwon and Charles Barkley, by then in Houston, I scored 18 points. My three-point play with 1:09 in the fourth—a jumper over the seven-foot-two Olajuwon—gave us a four-point lead and enabled us to hold off the physically superior Rockets.

In the morning after road games, no matter how tired we were from the previous night, the entire team would gather for breakfast together. When I tried to sneak some extra Z's, guys rang my room until I dragged myself out of bed and down to breakfast.

The first time I ordered Earl Grey tea, pandemonium broke out. No one, waiters included, had any idea what I was talking about. "Earl who?" Darrell laughed.

My teammates had never ordered anything wilder than Starbucks, and Darrell drank so much of that stuff that I was worried the caffeine would shake his little body to death.

It soon became a running gag. When waiters would look at me blankly as I tried to place my order, Bo joked, "What's the matter, don't you speak English?"

Then the guys started ordering it too, and I watched it sit, untouched and cold, through the meal. I'm not sure I won any converts to the golden elixir, but it was fun watching them make the effort, a subtle display of respect for my heritage and my place on the team.

I was shooting over 50 percent and generally dominating better-known players. So the entire team became superstitious about my tea. Panic would break out when I didn't get my pre-game dose, and my teammates made sure to order it for me in advance.

Other clubs were catching on. In Boston the ball boys earned a place in my heart by making sure there was a big thermos of the steaming stuff in my locker, including with the requisite skim milk. They should have known better: I lit up the Celtics that year.

After the *Orlando Sentinel* ran a big story on "the tea-drinking Brit," fans took to it as well. Before long I was receiving dozens of gifts of the stuff—homemade brews, tea cups, tankards, and rich biscuits.

The *Sentinel* went so far as to launch TEA WITH MEECH. In announcing the feature, the paper said, "Each week we'll enter the Technicolor mind of John Amaechi, the center who was raised in England and whose world extends far beyond the basketball court." (I always wondered whether the editors had actually meant "rainbow colored" mind. It was always my sense that reporters knew the truth about my sexuality but felt awkward raising the topic.)

Always happy to oblige the press, I'd sound off on a range of absurd topics. In one spot, they asked about my taste in television programs.

"I am a bit of a sci-fi buff," I said. "Call it escapism. Call it nerdy. I like what I like. My favorite shows are *Star Trek: The Next Generation* and *Voyager*. Among my new favorites are *Earth: Final Conflict*."

It was all part of the fun of a remarkable season.

●●●

Management loves to talk about building around "character" players. What they really mean is not admirable people, but athletes who won't screw up royally, who don't get caught with a gun under the car seat and a hooker on top of it. There's no evidence that real character has ever won a single game or sold a single hot dog, so standards tend to be rather low.

Ballplayers are neither the role models one would hope nor the sleazy thugs they are made out to be. Most are far more intelligent than people assume, but at the same time, I suppose it could be argued that they tend to have too many cars, jewelry, and girlfriends—a kind of American excess that is not particular to athletes. But they are most certainly not the kind of people you need to shield your children from.

That year, in fact, we were all about kids. During Magic Madness, a fan appreciation event at the arena, Bo Outlaw and Darrell Armstrong were their usual flamboyant selves, shooting around gleefully with a bunch of young people.

It's not at all common for players to be thrilled about these contractual duties. But I especially enjoyed it because it enabled me to continue my work with kids. I may have made it back to the NBA, but that was only half The Plan. Now I had to make sure I was benefiting someone other than myself.

Bo and Darrell were among the few who couldn't get enough of the game, and who allowed young fans to share their sense of joy. Rather than getting weighed down by the pressure of competition or caught up in ego, these guys appreciated that they were getting paid millions to play a kid's game.

My teammates that year were definitely drawn from the "good character" prototype. But that did not change their antipathy to my kind. Once, on a flight back to Orlando, one of my favorite guys launched into a diatribe along the lines of "homosexuals get what they deserve because they choose their immoral lifestyle."

I generally sat quietly on the plane, reading, snoozing, or typing on my laptop. Now my blood began to boil. I'd spent enough time among gay men in the past year to know for a fact they were no worse, and often better, than any group of human beings anywhere on earth. This guy was spouting recycled propaganda he'd read on some hate-filled web site or news page. His choice of words, mimicking the religious right, betrayed a total lack of independent thinking.

"Could you please explain why anyone would *choose* to be a member of the most maligned minority?" I asked, interrupting his verbal onslaught. "You're talking utter nonsense."

In America there's a lot of competition for most maligned. Post 9/11, I'd argue that gays have taken a back seat to Muslims. Or perhaps it's gay Muslims, facing double persecution, who have it worst of all. Or perhaps ranking is unnecessary. There's plenty of prejudice to go around.

At any rate, my comment halted the conversation. I went back to whatever I was doing, and I don't remember any more outbursts for the rest of that season, at least that I was privy to.

When it comes to team dynamics, challenging the prevailing (lack of) wisdom is always risky. However, I was in the starting lineup, playing significant minutes and contributing big time. I'd earned the right to speak my mind, even on a difficult topic. If teammates alienated me, they were alienating our playoff hopes (and those big post-season bonuses). Had I been in a more vulnerable position, I would have had little choice but to keep my opinions to myself.

In this case I felt confident speaking up on an issue, even though it was likely to raise serious suspicions about my sexual orientation. You didn't have to be a sociologist to read between the lines of the exchange: *Amaechi's queer.* I was taking a significant risk in allowing even the guessing game, and it is precisely that kind of concern that makes it so hard for gay athletes—or even their straight supporters—to speak up in any context, public or private.

This was my split-second calculation: There's a big difference between subtext and text, at least in this case. My teammates could speculate about my sexuality behind my back all they wanted, as long as it didn't affect the team or their respect for me as a leader.

At least some guys wondered. But the only guy to mention it was Monty Williams. Not long after the plane episode he said, "Meech, you never talk about *girls.*" It was unclear whether this was a question or a statement, but it was clear he was fishing. He seemed well intentioned, and for all I knew was looking for an opportunity to show support.

But I didn't feel particularly safe taking his bait, so I tried a somewhat neutral response. "I know," I answered. "I never talk about girls."

Of course, I spoke adoringly about my Mum, my sisters, and my female friends. But he was right—certainly not about girls the way some players did, all the time and in the most graphic of terms. (In Orlando, I actually had a very respectful set of teammates. The talk rarely descended into recitations of one-night stands and the objectification of various beautiful model types. Conversations got lewd, but stopped short of the ear-melting comments I heard at other stops.)

When the topic arose, my strategy was to remain vague. That way I would neither get caught in a lie nor be forced spend the rest of my career fending off gay-bashers. Trash talk is brutal enough without absorbing a steady stream of elbows to the ribs from 250-pound power forwards, followed closely by homophobic taunts.

One Canadian power forward called me a "fag" every time we were on the court together. I'm not sure it was based on anything more than the fact that my accent inflamed him, and the best he could come up with was that particular epithet.

Or maybe he was just trying to get under my skin.

Once again, my sexuality was relegated to the realm of fantasy. I rarely saw Darren, who was so far away that we'd broken it off. Other than my teammates, I had few friends in Orlando. I didn't know a single gay person. The most I could do was fancy from afar someone pretty I happened across.

Off court I hung out with Tariq Abdul-Wahid. On the surface, we couldn't have been more different—me the single British gay guy, he the married Muslim from France. (Born Olivie St. Jean, he converted to Islam and married a Muslim woman.) On a deeper level, we bonded. We were introspective Europeans in a foreign land who shared a passion for exploring cities, hanging out in cafés, and great conversation.

We debated everything from Islam, from which he drew great comfort and meaning, to politics, to European cities and the culture of sports. We skated around the issue of homosexuality, which he saw as a sin but harbored no hatred.

I enjoyed the fact that he took the time to educate me about his religious beliefs. I was enthralled by his dedication to his faith, something I felt about all religious people even when I disagreed with them.

On a day off during a road trip to Toronto, we took the subway, where a friendly ticket-seller asked us where we were from and promptly presented us with passes to tour the city. We made our way around Toronto, exploring, ending up at Morton's Steakhouse. I swear we ate everything in the place, but avoided my customary red wine accompaniment because, as a Muslim, he did not drink. We talked in a combination of English and my bad French until they shut the place down and kicked us out.

Shortly before he was traded, he said to me in his French lilt, "Meech, you are the only person I have ever met who is an expert at not fitting in no matter where you go."

I think he meant it as a compliment.

●••

Orlando is a booming metropolis. But it also home to Walt Disney World and the whole family mythology built up around it. So players must be particularly careful about where they're seen and how they're perceived.

It seemed my teammates went to great lengths—like me, but for very different reasons—to avoid the possibility of being caught in youthful indiscretions, fearing the usual litany of scandals, from unwanted pregnancies to sexual assault charges to the whole sex-with-prostitutes routine. We were focused.

Temptation is the ballplayer's constant companion, particularly for the straight ones. The combination of wealth, athleticism, and celebrity is a powerful aphrodisiac. Basketball in particular, with its indoor arenas and courtside seats, creates the illusion of intimacy between players and fans. Clad in revealing uniforms (no matter how baggy they have become), players are half naked on the floor, our sweat showering the stands.

On those rare occasions when I ventured out to clubs with my teammates, I was amazed at boldness of gorgeous young women. It became predictable: They would approach, touch, and chat provocatively, and then leave their phone numbers scribbled on the back of cocktail napkins, stuffed into my pants pocket.

The players' attitude could be summed up as live and let live. (Except same-sex liaisons, which always invited condemnation.) We all knew the score, who was shagging whom, but they didn't reveal much beyond the general braggadocio. A raised eyebrow, a wry smile, a well-timed joke perhaps. But it was, with some exceptions, considered uncool to comment directly on another man's business. Which suited me just fine.

On my way home after games, I'd drive by a gay bar on Orange Avenue. It was then that I most desired to morph into an ordinary gay man, at peace with himself and his world, slip quietly onto a barstool, sip a gin and tonic, chat with other ordinary guys. Just like back home in Manchester.

Sometimes being six-foot-ten and being semi-famous can be a bitch.

I settled for gliding slowly past the bar, gazing through the window as patrons, frenetic dance beats, and pulsing light drifted out of the doors and into the night.

●●●

On the last day of the season, we were eliminated from the play-off hunt in Milwaukee. It was disappointing, to be sure, mostly because I would miss the fun of playing with this great group of guys and showing the world our stuff on a bigger stage.

But we were justifiably proud of what we'd accomplished, finishing 41–41, trampling teams with whom we shouldn't even have shared the same hardwood. The Lakers were the only play-off team we did not defeat. (Shaq made sure of that.)

We were not the only ones who felt that way. Doc was rewarded with the 1999–2000 NBA Coach of the Year. The rest of us had our stature—and contract leverage—boosted. But most of all, we'd had the pleasure of treating fans to a fantastic year of gritty, fundamental ball. "A stunning reminder that a loveable band of low-rent overachievers still can thrive in an age of dot.com, over-valued superstars," *Sentinel* basketball writer Tim Povtak put it in an ode to our season.

Having thwarted management's plan, it was going to be a fas-cinating off-season. I would become a free agent the day after our last game, likely to draw some serious suitors. (The *Sentinel* termed my contract situation "Peachy for Amaechi.")

Rumors abounded that the Magic would sign Tim Duncan, relegating me to backup status or the free agent market. Under labor rules, the team could only offer me a 30 percent raise. But I knew I'd take less than market value to stay with this terrific city, this fearless bunch of guys, and the chance to make another playoff run.

Would general manager John Gabriel and owner Rich DeVos jettison this crew they'd assembled for a bunch of big names, as they had planned? Or would they stick with Heart & Hustle over Rich & Famous?

CHAPTER 18 ●●●] Go West, Young Man

For a free agent center, there's nothing quite like the sight of Phil Jackson pulling up on his black Harley. It's a pretty good indication that you are wanted, big time. Words are almost beside the point.

Over waffles at the Beverly Wilshire Hotel, I chatted with Jackson and Lakers GM Mitch Kupchak—a pretty good big man in his own right.

The previous night I'd enjoyed dinner at a little hole-in-the-wall Italian place with another Laker legend, Jerry West, so there wasn't much serious business to conduct at the Wilshire. As vice president, West had laid out the team's plans for me over red wine and steaming bowls of pasta.

The brain trusts' message was clear: They had seen me improve, they had been impressed by my work ethic, fundamental play, and the way I flourished as a role player. They were confident I would thrive in their system.

I was to back up Shaq, save him a little wear and tear, contribute my customary 7 to 11 points per game. Pull down a few boards, take up some space in the paint. Root for the stars. Contribute to team chemistry. It was far from superstardom, but not a bad day job.

Among these men there was quiet, unspoken certainty not just about my role but about the larger mission: replicating the dynasty Jackson and Jordan had created in Chicago. And I was to play a role, albeit a complementary one.

There were many things I wanted to talk about with the bearded, leather-jacketed Jackson. I would benefit from playing for a coach who sought me out in part because he saw parallels in my own cerebral approach. But for once, I was nearly mute as I sipped nervously at my Earl Grey, picked at my waffles, and glanced uncomfortably around the impossibly posh setting. It was a long way from middle-class Manchester.

From there I was whisked in a limo to the Lakers' practice facility near LAX, where I met again with West, who was in his last summer as GM. As I walked to his office, we passed a practice facility where young hopefuls were stretching and waiting for a scrimmage. They stared back, and it dawned on me that just two years ago I'd been their position, on the outside looking in. I saw the way they looked at me, tired eyes tinged with envy, and I have to admit I took some small satisfaction from it. Now I'd achieved their dream and mine, an established pro, secure in my NBA future.

I almost succumbed to the cliché and pinched myself. Having just met with one of the greatest coaches of all time, I was on my way to meet once again with one of history's greatest players, not to mention GMs. (He'd just announced his resignation but was finishing up old business.)

Bill had already outlined the offer, but West wanted to make clear what was on the table. "We're prepared to sign you right now," he said, looking me in the eye as I sat down in a huge leather couch in his office. "I am leaving L.A. soon, so I want there to be no misunderstanding about what's on the table for you here. We would like you to sign with us. We can offer you our maximum. We know it will leave you underpaid in upcoming years if you continue to improve, but this is what can be done right now."

I could barely believe my ears. It was simultaneously the bluntest and most generous offer I'd ever received. A decade earlier I had been the ultimate outcast, an awkward, overgrown nerd a continent away who didn't know the Lakers from a lake.

Now I was being offered a contract to play for a celebrated franchise by a living legend who thought I might be even more valuable than they could afford under the league's salary cap: a cool $17 million spread over six years.

I didn't need to be sold. I adored the place: the warm but dry climate, the short trip to my Scottsdale home, the sprawling, old-fashioned neighborhoods like Hollywood, the glorious multiculturalism. Los Angeles even boasted one of my favorite gay meccas, a huge outdoor patio at the Abbey on Santa Monica (not that I planned on getting photographed there). It was a place I'd already nervously checked out a few times, without incident, but I realized that if I signed, I'd be a lot less anonymous there.

I checked out a bunch of homes in Hermosa Beach, a short drive from the arena where I could get a view of the Pacific and some privacy.

I was well aware of the stakes. You didn't have to be Marv Albert to predict a Chicago-like series of championship rings. With Kobe and Shaq, a bevy of talented role players, all under the leadership of the Zen master himself, the pieces were in place.

My place in the game's history would be secure as long as I didn't rock the Lakers' boat. My play would continue to grow under Jackson's and Shaq's tutelage. My doubters back home could never again say I hadn't made an impact. My financial future would be secured, and then some.

Best of all, my charities would be enhanced, as would my ability to sell the game back in Britain and to reach out to troubled kids everywhere.

The truth is I seriously considered blurting out, "MY GOD, YES" right there, even though there were many offers piling up on my agent's desk, some of which matched or exceeded the L.A. offer. As I flew back to Orlando, my heart was in shambles. I wanted to sign my name on the dotted line as badly as I'd wanted anything in my life. But I wanted to stay with my teammates in Orlando, too.

When I called Bill and told him of my dilemma, he was beside himself, practically questioning my sanity. He reminded me that under an arcane league salary rule known as the "veteran midline exception," the Magic, even if they did want to keep me, were limited to offering a 30 percent raise over the $380,000 I'd been paid the previous year. They could not compete with the Lakers' offer until the following season.

Uki and Muriel were all in favor of it. Even my teammates, having been in similar situations and understanding the enormity of the offer, could not have objected to my abandoning them.

But there was another reason for my reticence. My heart was in Orlando, and not just with my stellar bunch of teammates and coach.

CHAPTER 19 ●●●] Family Values

The Magic's arena in downtown Orlando is divided in two. There are team facilities, closed to the public, and, on the other side, a private membership gym, equipped with weight rooms, indoor track, and a court where anyone can shoot hoops or find a pick-up game.

In those uncertain weeks before I'd officially made the team, I lacked the clearance to work out in the team facility, so I'd head over to the public side to keep sharp in the rare free time I had.

That's where I got to know some local kids. I was practicing my jumper one day when two teenagers sidled up and started chatting. With their military haircuts and wide, friendly faces, they could have been the brothers they turned out to be—Martin and Jeff Jones, aged 16 and 17.

They had no idea who I was. Nobody in that city did. I couldn't have been elected dog catcher at that point. I was wearing my regular workout duds, lacking even a spare Orlando uniform. The only way anyone could have identified me was when Bo Outlaw showed up and spoke to me familiarly, tipping them off that I might be "one of the guys." Of course, my height and skill level were clues, but I could easily have been one of those washed-up former college stars who are always hanging around gyms. (In fact, some might have said that's exactly what I was at that point.)

I take pride in the fact that kids have always felt comfortable approaching me, no matter where I happened to be in my career—top, bottom or, usually, somewhere in between. While I may look intimidating to adults, kids seem to know almost instinctively that I'm just a big softy.

At first our meeting was unremarkable, beginning with the usual grunts, pre-game handshakes, and exchanges of first names that come with pulling together a pick-up team. Even in pick-up ball, I played to win. But I also knew the kids were in it mostly for the fun, so I tried to make sure I kept them involved in the game while I got the cardio workout I needed.

Between games, people commented on my "funny accent" and this became, as ever, the opening to a bit of my life story—though I generally have a little too much British reserve to spill my guts right away.

To me, Martin and Jeff were just regular kids, except for the fact that they had an "old" quality, a coarseness teenagers under strain increasingly convey. What I didn't know, and didn't learn until years later, was that Martin knew that day I was what he called "the one" because I remembered his name. Since hearing that, I've tried never to underestimate the power of making a personal connection, no matter how trivial it might seem at the time.

The Jones boys, I learned, shared an apartment not far from the arena, and their parents, both of whom worked out of town, were rarely around. They were on their own, attending a local private high school, where they both starred on the basketball team. It wasn't an ideal arrangement, but it was one the family required at the moment.

After a dozen or so meetings, we struck up a friendship. I'd made the squad, so I often gave them my courtside tickets. Afterwards, they'd wait around in the family suite for me to shower and dress, and we'd head to a place downtown where four or five of my teammates and I would devour the biggest cheeseburgers known to man.

On off days, we made a beeline for Sweet Tomatoes, a soup and salad buffet. No buffet place can hope for a profit with my family around, and had the management had any sense, it would have shuttered the moment they saw us coming down the street.

Then, school pals in tow (and sometimes a teammate and his wife and kids), they'd pile into my car and head to Epcot Center, compliments of Disney's deal with the Magic in which players get unlimited passes.

I'm ride-phobic, so we spent more time at the nation-themed parks, doing what I do best: eat and drink—mint tea in Morocco, fish and chips in England. We loved the parades and the fireworks displays over the artificial lake, and just people-watching.

I knew firsthand the value of family excursions as an antidote to the stresses of childhood, and I worked hard to provide a similar experience to my "kids."

Because Mum worked so much when I was growing up, our annual summer camping trip was our favorite time. Mum would wake us before sunrise, a Herculean task. She'd pack a lunch of chopped salad, ham and cheese sandwiches, and flasks of tea and juice, arming her with the ability to ignore our incessant demands to stop at greasy spoons along the journey.

The two-hour journey to North Wales from Stockport seemed an eternity. Mum punctuated the trips with the usual diversionary games of I Spy, and a collection of soundtrack cassettes—from *Bedknobs and Broomsticks* and *The Aristocats* to *Mary Poppins* and *Jungle Book*. We would sing along in harmony until Mum's wavering falsetto would ruin it. "Muuuuum, you're spoiling it!" we'd cry.

On all these holidays we three kids donned blue quilted vests to keep us warm when we went ice-skating or into deep underground caves. Mum sewed on cloth badges from each of the attractions we'd visited. After a few years, the badges had taken over the vests, each marking a cherished memory. Even today, I have a mental picture of Mum, peering over her glasses while we played, as she looked up from the historical novel she was reading that week.

I could never re-create those magical days completely, but I certainly could try. And the times when I saw the joy in the eyes of Martin and Jeff were some of the proudest moments of my life. Typical teenaged boys, they did their bored and unimpressed look. But before long they couldn't help betraying their enthusiasm, expressed in the form of smiles, yelps, and high-fives.

After the season ended, Martin, a pretty good ballplayer in his own right, joined me in Manchester at my summer basketball camp. (Jeff stayed in Orlando, where he had a job.) He stayed at

Muriel's house, and spent a lot of time poking around a country he'd only seen in movies.

During one game, he badly sprained his ankle. I sat by his side as the ambulance raced to the hospital. He was writhing in pain. I'd had more than my share of injuries, so although I knew he'd be fine, I suffered along with him. Pain, especially the kind you haven't experienced before, is scary because you are never quite sure when it will go away.

The paramedic gave him laughing gas, and he went from yelping to grinning and giggling and back again. I watched his face the whole time and only one tear fell from his eyes. It dripped down his face so slowly that it looked like the force of his will held it back.

After the laughing gas wore off, Martin turned serious. "Can me and Jeff move in with you?" he asked.

The timing indicated that I was being manipulated. Who can say no to a kid in agony? Yet I didn't feel manipulated because the request came from such a vulnerable place.

I was flattered. The boys were looking for a mentor and an adult guardian on a permanent basis. They had chosen to trust me. I'd mentored more than 40 teenagers since college, so expanding one such relationship felt like the natural next step.

It wasn't the best time to discuss the pitfalls of such an arrangement. I was a free-agent; Bill was already receiving calls inquiring about my availability, including the one from Jerry West. If Orlando didn't come through with an offer, I would have my choice of half a dozen teams and multi-million-dollar offers.

"You are always welcome in my house, Martin, no matter what, but I can't guarantee I will be in Orlando next year," I explained as gently as I could. "Let's talk about it when we get back there."

I knew it would take a lot to drag me away from Orlando. After six years as a vagabond ballplayer, peddling my wares around the globe, I'd found a home—and the family I'd always wanted to go with it.

The responsibility of kids made staying around all the more appealing. It seemed all the money in the world couldn't compensate for the joy of being needed. It would have been unfair to pick up and move across the country and either leave them behind or disrupt their lives by bringing them with me. They were happily ensconced in their schools, and they'd be going from living a few hundred miles away from their biological parents to a few thousand.

At the same time, there were business ramifications I had to take seriously, consequences that went far beyond my own financial future. I'd dreamed for years of reinvigorating British basketball so more kids could share the opportunity I enjoyed. Joe Forber and I were about to break ground on the Amaechi Basketball Centre in Manchester, a state-of-the-art basketball facility we hoped would draw kids from around the country.

We envisioned a vast network of similar gyms stretching from coast to coast. Kids of all ages and economic backgrounds would be able to participate equally, supported by the best coaching money could buy. Over the long haul, we knew, this would not only help thousands of ordinary young people reach their potential, but would produce some world-class talent. (It was cool being the only Brit in the NBA, but I didn't want to hold the distinction for any longer than I had to.)

In building the first center in Manchester, I'd pledged $500,000 of my own money, with the balance of $1 million to be raised through other private donations. I'd already spent $120,000 more than Orlando had paid me for the whole season.

I might have to pitch in far more. Seventeen million of the Lakers' dollars would have bought a lot of hardwood and Puma hightops for the kids, while keeping me in nice cars for the rest of my life.

All of which contributed to my excruciating dilemma, a dilemma on which The Plan seemed at first to shed little light. I was supposed to behave in a way that would make my mentors proud, in a way that would make me proud of myself. It seemed a Hobson's choice between the promises I'd made to Martin and Jeff and the assurances of great riches—riches that would make my own life secure but, more important, would benefit young athletes back home.

But on another level, I knew that was a false choice. In either case I'd be all right financially, and Martin and Jeff were certainly strong enough to survive and thrive, even if I moved away. As Mum had made clear, the real choice was about what I wanted, about my soul in the dark.

I spent three sleepless nights sprawled on my couch drinking pot after pot of tea and mulling over every aspect of the decision.

My mind told me to take the L.A. deal, but my heart remained in Orlando. When heart and mind are in conflict, the heart wins.

Then again, perhaps the overdose of Earl Grey was making me hallucinate. That's certainly what everyone would say if I turned down joining a club that was on the verge of becoming one of the best teams in NBA history.

●••

Before I made a decision, I needed to hear what the Magic had to say.

Although GM John Gabriel could not offer me L.A. money, he flew me to billionaire owner Rich DeVos's private mansion in Palm Beach so the noble man could personally assure me that he'd make up for the difference between the contracts the following year, when there would be no arbitrary limit on my salary.

It was a bit of a *Charlie's Angels* moment. DeVos himself wasn't there. Instead, I was ushered into his study, where Gabe and I chatted until the phone rang. Gabe answered and handed the phone to me. I spoke to Rich for no more than 15 minutes, basking in his words and ideas.

Concepts of "family," "rewarding trust," "never forgetting loyalty" poured forth. Looking back now, had this been college recruiting, I would have hung up. But I wanted to believe his words more than anything in the world.

DeVos personally gave me his word they would "take care" of me in the future, and that I had "nothing to worry about." As part of the "Magic family," he assured me that I'd always have a place there.

Gabriel said essentially the same thing. "John, your game would have to fall to pieces for us not to bring you back next year."

By taking a chance on me the previous season, jettisoning two expensive vets in the process, Gabriel and DeVos had given me a new life in the NBA. I had put in the hard work, made the sacrifices, but they gave me an opportunity at a time when few would. My sense of loyalty and integrity told me I owed them another year.

Although I was passing up the opportunity of a lifetime, I trusted these men would return the favor. I would sacrifice one year of a hefty contract, but I would still be financially set and my future would be assured.

In July, Bill reluctantly declined the Lakers offer and I signed on Orlando's dotted line. My web site was promptly was flooded with 3,000 e-mails from Lakers fans telling me I must be out of my fucking English mind.

Perhaps they were right.

I celebrated my decision by throwing myself into training for the following season and even further into the lives of these two fantastic kids.

CHAPTER 20 ●●●] Home at Last

Once I'd re-upped with the Magic, I bought a house in Maitland, a planned community not far from our practice venue, the RDV Sportsplex. It was just a few miles from Payne Stewart's mansion, soon to be purchased by Tracy McGrady, though nowhere near as grand.

Mine was one of those sprawling places you seen on MTV's *Cribs*, the show where athletes and rock stars show off their fleet of cars, overstuffed leather furniture, and a warren of gaudily decorated, underused rooms.

In fact, my house was featured on the British version of the series. But it was no show place, as it would soon overflow with my new family. Muriel would be joining me, as would Helen, a close friend from England who had taken a job in Orlando.

Before Jeff and Martin moved in, I had a long conversation with their parents. Not only did they approve of the living situation, they were eager to legally formalize my surrogate parenthood. With the private guardianship we ended up signing, I would be there for the boys legally and financially as well emotionally. They were genuinely relieved that they would be well provided for.

I'll never forget the expressions on Jeff and Martin's faces as they crossed the threshold of the new house for the first time. Their eyes sort of bugged out, like cartoon characters. Even though they were losing access to the pool and massive hot tub of my old apartment complex, they were floored at the grandeur of the new place.

By some strange twist of fate, I was no longer just another member of the Orlando Magic; I was a parent to two sometimes unruly teenaged boys. I would be at their school when they were having trouble, in the stands at their basketball games, at their bedside when they were sick.

Imagine your ordinary family, only with a single half-Nigerian, half-British, six-foot-ten dad. With the brassy, loyal Helen and Muriel thrown in, we certainly didn't look like the Waltons, even if we more often than not behaved like them.

I was on the road a lot, so having Muriel and Helen around was a big help. But it also sometimes created a crisis of authority. While Jeff and Martin responded to my guidance, the need to listen to Muriel and Helen caused some friction. They viewed them as akin to step-parents moving in, and they felt like it spoiled the male bonding we had enjoyed.

Overall the arrangement worked, though. My heart still swells when I look at the pictures from Jeff's high school graduation, where we were all together.

Jeff and Martin had homework, so they were required to stay in most weeknights, except during home games, when they were fixtures on the Magic sidelines. I limited their television watching and did my best to help them when they got stuck with social studies, history, and English.

My cooking ability was sorely tested. In the morning, I'd scramble them some eggs or boil some oatmeal if it was early enough in the season to drag my aching body out of bed. If not, Muriel and Helen would make sure everyone was fed and, no matter how late I'd gotten in from the road, I'd make sure I was up to see them off to school.

Naturally, I brought a bit of Europe to parenting. They were allowed a glass of wine or beer with dinner. The point was to demystify the experience so they would feel less need to experiment with their friends. Lord knows, given my teenaged drinking exploits, I was in no position to preach. (They were, however, forbidden from drinking and driving. Even liberal Europeans have their limits.)

Not long after he moved in, Martin got a girlfriend and I talked with them about staying safe to protect their futures by avoiding STDs and unwanted pregnancies. I stayed away from the Jerry Falwell-esque moralizing parenting that has become so prevalent in America. My goal was to arm them with information so they could make good decisions on their own. One of the worst mistakes in parenting is to make the forbidden seem appealing.

I gave the boys a lot of rope, and they occasionally stretched it to the breaking point. On weekends they were allowed to stay out until midnight. One Friday night before an early afternoon game, I heard them come in around 2 a.m. as I lay awake. I was steamed. It wasn't so much that they had cost me sleep on a game day. I was angry that they had not let me know they would be late or bothered to explain why.

Rather than scream at them, I hoped they could figure out why I was upset. After finding my cool neutrality too much to handle, they went to Muriel, who told them why I was upset. After they apologized, we were all relieved. They had shown they understood why responsibility was important, and they got that I hadn't stopped caring for them just because they had disappointed me.

The lesson stuck. After practice one day, I pulled into the driveway and pushed the garage door opener. As the door slid open, I could see a pair of feet, then legs, then the full Jeff, looking like the world had come to an end.

"What happened?" I sighed as I pulled myself out of my car, fearing a burned down kitchen, schoolyard brawl, or bad report card. It turned out that Jeff broken the lid of my Spode teapot while cleaning it. He knew I loved my china, and feared I'd be crushed.

I was anything but. In fact, I told him I appreciated that he'd taken responsibility for it. It was a sign that he was heeding my messages about taking responsibility, no matter the consequences. I knew that we were developing as a family by Jeff's response to this little incident.

The vulnerability worked both ways. Martin got a concussion after being knocked on the head at school. I put him to bed and checked on him all night. I sat in the dark, listening to him snore, periodically placing my hand on his forehead, ostensibly to check his temperature, but more to comfort myself than anything.

At one point I accidentally mashed his nose with my elbow. He yelped and rolled over, but never awakened.

My God I'm a terrible parent, I remember thinking. *I have no idea what I'm doing. I just mashed my kid in the face.*

I had to step into the living room to get some perspective, to realize that's how all parents feel at one point or another. They just have the advantage of starting a little earlier. I went back to Martin's room, where I waited until my eyes adjusted to the dark to make sure he was fine.

Only then could I sleep.

●●●

My friends comment on how unguarded I must have been to let these kids into my life. Frankly, I've never had a lot to be pompous about. When we first met, I was staying at a cheap hotel and didn't even have access to the players' locker room and courts. My NBA future was tenuous. Although I was a ballplayer, I was hardly a household name.

There were few raised eyebrows about our arrangement. When it did come up, race was the issue. Here was a black father, a highly visible black father no less, raising two boys who looked, with their spikey hair and wife-beater T-shirts, one part redneck and one part skinhead. Americans are accustomed to the opposite configuration, seeing abandoned black kids as the ones needing adoption.

As a half-black kid raised by a white mother, interracial parenting felt not just ordinary but natural. And it never became an issue for Martin or Jeff. Anyway, we were enjoying the experience far too much to worry about what others thought. To me it wasn't important that other people understood. I never felt it was my job to elaborate. Besides, my reputation as a Big Brother preceded me.

Doc was supportive, and Jeff and Martin became fixtures around the team. When I was on the court or in the locker room, the players' wives looked after them. My teammates, some of whom were fathers themselves, were supportive, seeing it as just another facet of who I was.

●••

The guardianship was a private arrangement with Martin and Jeff's parents. But had I gone through an agency, I likely would have been denied, unless I'd lied about my sexual orientation. Florida was one of several states to ban gay people from serving as foster or adoptive parents, apparently based on the notion that they are poor role models.

Although many of the people making these arguments are parents themselves, you would never know it. Anyone who has been around kids knows that sexual orientation has as much to do with parenting ability as dunking prowess. Parenting is about empathy, kindness, consistency, authority, and unconditional love—qualities that are evenly distributed along gay-straight lines. Gay people are already raising kids, and I don't think we are about to sprout a whole generation of raging queers. (Not that there would be anything wrong with that.)

Some foster parents will only take in kids of a certain age, of a certain size, or with a clean bill of health. Others want a particular race, religion, or sexual orientation. I took in Jeff and Martin, too old for official adoption, because they asked me to.

My sexuality was a non-issue anyway. I never sat down and said, "Jeff, Martin, I'm gay." We talked honestly and openly about everything. But I never felt it was appropriate to discuss my own sexuality, so I avoided dating entirely that year. Actually, I didn't have to avoid it—it had never really been an option anyway. Perhaps I was still a bit uncomfortable with the idea myself.

My priority was clear: I was trying to parent two young men, and that needed to be my focus, not my own romantic life.

When I finally said the words, "I'm gay" to them several years later, it didn't exactly arrive as a bombshell. Whenever they had asked about my own dating life, even when the were teens, they were careful to use gender-neutral terms to be sure to neither offend me nor force me into a premature revelation.

Basically it was irrelevant. They just wanted someone to be there for them, no matter what. I was happy to oblige.

CHAPTER 21 ●●●] Betrayal

By the time the 2000 training camp rolled around, I was raring to go. The Magic missed out on Tim Duncan, who opted to stay in San Antonio. Instead, the team pulled off a basketball coup, signing both Grant Hill *and* Tracy McGrady, two of the games' flashiest and most prolific scorers, to identical $93 million contracts. We also acquired Andrew DeClercq, who would handle the power forward spot and help shore up one of our weaknesses, rebounding.

The new talent was spellbinding. But it also meant we'd have to jettison some of our stalwarts, some of the guys who'd exemplified Heart & Hustle. Ben was gone, traded to Detroit, where he would blossom under Larry Brown. Chucky Atkins was gone as well. Bo and Darrell returned. We all still worked hard. But it wasn't the same.

With the introduction of a star system, we lost a lot of what had made us so special the previous year. The role players had smaller roles as Tracy took control of the offense, especially after Grant re-injured his left ankle, which he'd broken the previous year.

Tracy was one the most physically gifted athletes with whom I'd ever shared a floor. Everything on display on those highlight reels is even more impressive up close: the soaring dunks, the soft three-point shots, the ability to create. He's a one-man team.

But at 21 he lacked the work ethic we had established the previous year, and his punctuality left a lot to be desired. His play was more Tracy and less team. Unlike Michael Jordan, he didn't make anyone better except himself. He was a superstar among anti-superstars, and that created a low-grade tension that shadowed us all year.

The transition from scrappy overachievers to star-studded run-and-gunners was rocky. Tracy elevated our play by improving our offensive firepower, but at the expense of so much we'd achieved.

Players knew it. Fans knew it. Opponents knew it. The Magic was gone.

Since we lacked a big-name center, Michael Doleac and I were counted on to play the majority of minutes in the middle, though my scoring opportunities diminished. There was no way Darrell would be allowed to look for me *first*.

I started out where I'd left off. I scored 35 points in a pre-season game, a career high. I went for 28 against Portland. Big men were still struggling to adjust to my ambidextrous low-post style. Double-teamed, I worked on my passing to take advantage of the mismatches it created.

Then my play went south of Key West. I wasn't getting as many touches so I couldn't find my scoring rhythm. When I did get the ball in decent position, I pressed, leading to bad shots, lousy footwork, and turnovers. By November I was averaging 8.8 points a game and shooting just 37 percent, about 10 percent below where I'd been the previous year. It got to the point where I would pass the ball rather than look to score, which wasn't helping the team.

The coaches knew I wasn't getting the ball as much as I once did. We had a new focal point to the offense, but that is little solace when you are trying to pull yourself out off a slump.

Michael Jordan slumps. Tracy McGrady slumps. We all slump. You just have to grind your way out. My skills hadn't slipped; I simply wasn't executing. The end of an unproductive season loomed in my nightmares, and everything told me the honeymoon was over. The brother-in-arms of the season before become the quirky single uncle who is not invited to the family reunions.

Because I was coming off a breakout year at the relatively advanced NBA age of 29, I was unlikely to get the kind of forbearance vets get. I'd fallen into the vicious cycle of pressure and poor performance that's every ballplayer's nightmare.

It became a mini Orlando crisis. It seemed the entire town was talking about my struggles. Amaechi's a "compulsive thinker," wrote *Sentinel* basketball writer David Whitley in November. "His brainwaves are constantly humming, which is why he's probably the only NBA player working on a doctorate in child psychology. What makes it worse is he's got so much to think about these days."

That was the generous way to put it. There are plenty of smart basketball players, and most of them were not slumping. Plenty of guys had a lot on their mind.

Doc told me to shoot my way out of the slump, McGrady be damned. So, matched up against Rasheed Wallace in Portland, I hoisted 24 shots, scoring 27 points. The explosive Wallace kept me so busy on the boards and on defense that it forced me back into the flow of the game, where I could forget my troubles. My shots started to fall, and I played one of the game's best big men to a standoff.

The relief was temporary. Few knew the full story of my family and the sacrifices I'd made to stay in Orlando. There was something preying on my mind, albeit subconsciously at first. I couldn't quite shake the suspicion that the Magic would fail to live up to their promise to bring me back the next year, that I'd allowed myself to be bamboozled. I had nothing more than verbal promises, which, as Bill was the first to remind me, are about as valuable as second-round draft picks. I was so eager to believe Gabriel and DeVos that I failed to fully consider the possibility that something could go terribly wrong.

My worst fear was that the team would use any slump, any weakness or injury, no matter how temporary or minor, as a pretext to renege on a deal. The more I thought this way, the harder it was to excel.

There was no one thing that confirmed my fears. It wasn't as though I had access to an internal memo that said LET'S SHAFT AMAECHI. It was more like death by a million tiny cuts, a series of little things that demonstrated something was very, very wrong.

Gabriel, for one, stopped speaking to me. It's never a good sign when the general manager ignores you. The media office stopped featuring me in campaigns. Team officials stopped talking about me when discussing future plans.

In England we have a term for it: "constructive dismissal." You are placed in an untenable position, a position so precarious that you feel compelled to depart of your own accord, saving executives the ugliness of having to fire you.

I told myself it couldn't be happening, that I was imagining things. I tried to put my suspicions aside, funnelling my energy back into my game. But it was tough. Even the slightest distraction can send your confidence into a tailspin, and they didn't get any bigger than this one.

I reacted by withdrawing. On team flights the previous year or in the locker room, I was invariably surrounded by teammates, laughing, trash-talking, chatting. Now I was so gloomy that guys refused to sit near me, letting me brood by myself.

I found it hard, impossibly hard, to play well for a franchise that raised doubts about my future with the team after I'd sacrificed so much to stay. That I was popular with teammates, the media, and the community didn't help. It only made me feel I was letting down an entire city.

Darrell put it best: "You're getting screwed, man."

I was situated below the guillotine, waiting for Gabriel's order for the blade to drop.

Then came the national anthem flap.

I'd developed a pre-game ritual of burying my head in a towel in order to create some private space where I could get into a game "zone." It sometimes overlapped with the playing of the national anthem.

When a few fans noticed this, I started to get all the usual nationalistic bull via e-mail. "Get out of the country," "Go home," and other nasty epithets arrived in my inbox.

What these ignoramuses didn't realize, of course, is that while I was raised in Manchester, I was actually born in Boston. I was as American as the e-mailers. And I meant no disrespect.

I admire players, like baseball slugger Carlos Delgado, who have chosen to speak their mind by refusing to stand for the national anthem. In 1996, Mahmoud Abdul-Rauf, a Muslim guard for Denver, created a stir when he refused to stand to protest U.S. foreign policy. It seems to me that this is the kind of speech we need more of, not less.

I applaud those who protest. I, too, oppose much of U.S. foreign policy. But it was not my intention to make a statement. It was merely my chance to meditate, a time when a lot of guys find ways to get locked in.

Why is it when a fan slurps Coke and munches on popcorn through the anthem it's okay, but when I rest my head in a towel it's "hating America"?

It was a tempest in my teapot, and most people accepted my explanation. But it was yet another distraction in a season full of them.

My only consolation was off court. Our family life was constantly in motion, and the energy rubbed off. Away from basketball, I would perk up the way a depressed person can still be happy with a temporary change of scenery. Yet I couldn't hide my pain from Jeff and Martin. I'd tried to show them that integrity is important, that a man is only as good as his word, and they could see that the value I placed in such decency had been shaken.

They protested the way kids protest bad deals by their favorite teams: by refusing to watch the team, even on free TV, and by discarding their beloved Magic gear.

I didn't want to deprive them of their fandom, but I wasn't in any position to object, either.

Given the relationship I had with Rich DeVos, the looming sense of rejection felt particularly painful. The previous year he'd found me at my locker and told me he was aware of "all my charity work," with school kids and the Orlando Museum of Art, and he appreciated the goodwill I brought back to the franchise.

At the team's Black Tie and Tennies Charity Gala toward the end of the season, the team presents a community service award. Darrell got it the previous year, deservedly. The guy has more energy and love to share than the Energizer bunny and the Dali Lama together.

As I stood there in my tux waiting for the announcement this year, it occurred to me that if I won the award, it might make management's treachery a little easier to take.

The award went to Grant Hill, who, among other things, had given a $1 million endowment to Duke University, the kind of largess only someone with his contract could afford. Grant was a worthy recipient. He was making a huge amount of money—$19 million that season—but was beset by injuries, and he suited up for only a dozen games or so. A lot of guys would have laughed all the way to the bank. But Grant was clearly uncomfortable about not being able to contribute on the court. So he strove to play the role of good teammate and citizen, and the award reflected that.

When the award was announced, DeVos, sitting behind me, leaned over and said, "John, you should have gotten it."

I'm not sure he was right, but it was indicative of the kind of relationship I thought I had with the man.

We did improve incrementally that year, making the playoffs, where we got smoked in the first round. A few days later, Gabriel, who hadn't said a word to me in some time, came up and promised, "Don't worry, we'll sort you out as soon as we can. You're our first priority."

I wasn't holding my breath. It was the first and last time I heard from him that season, and he didn't even have the decency to return Bill's calls. The team never made any attempt to keep me around. I was being shown the door.

Basically, it came down to the bottom line. I had a small contract; to keep me would require a big contract, and the suits figured that if Doleac, already under contract for another year, could contribute seven points a game, why did they need to give me the big contract they'd dangled to get me to sign for less?

Looking back, the vague assurance from DeVos that I "was family and would be treated like family" should have been a tip-off. It left him way too much deniability.

On one of my last days in Orlando, I marched into Gabriel's office to confront him. He sat there with a poker face, denying everything. "This is *not* the kind of club that makes promises based on character"—exactly the reverse of the line he'd fed me the previous year.

The sacrifices I'd made for the franchise meant nothing. But Gabriel wasn't as clever as he thought. Even insensitive people betray their guilt, and Gabriel was no exception. He refused to look me in the eye.

DeVos was not around the arena much, so I scrawled a plaintive letter asking for an explanation. Again, no response. All he had to do was admit he'd changed his mind and apologize, and I would move on, satisfied that he'd at least leveled with me.

What made the situation even more galling was that DeVos had founded Amway on "Christian" principles and wrote books about business integrity. Safe to say I wouldn't be picking up his latest: *Compassionate Capitalism: People Helping People Help Themselves.*

No matter how DeVos and Gabriel justified their actions, there was no way around the fact I didn't want to face: I had to leave my family and my adopted city.

All was not lost. I was still in line for a big contract, so I couldn't expect anyone to feel sorry for me (even if part of me wanted that). No matter how much money you make, having to leave a home you worked hard to create, a future you held dear, is never easy.

The hardship of the transition was softened by the fact that Jeff had already begun his freshman year at Central Florida University and Martin was one semester away. They wanted to move with me, but that didn't seem wise. Having been on their own for much of their adolescence, they were streetwise kids. It wasn't a good idea to uproot their college plans now that they were on the right track.

I promised to fly them around the country to see me play and hang out whenever they were on break. Helen was returning to Manchester, and Muriel would be moving, too.

In the free-agent market, I wasn't sizzling like the previous year but I was still generating heat. L.A. was now out of the running, scared off by my down season. Chicago, rebuilding post-Jordan and Jackson, made a strong bid. But Utah had sniffed around my first free agency, and it had put in another call to Bill. With its tradition of basketball excellence and veteran ballplayers like Karl Malone and John Stockton, Utah seemed an ideal match, a sort of junior version of the Lakers.

Having been burned once, I made sure to ask a lot of questions about my role, how I might fit into the system, and the city. I was told I'd play a lot of center and back up Malone. I'd always played well against my idol (one of the reasons the team was interested), and now I would give him a breather at power forward—nothing less than an honor.

Coach Jerry Sloan told me he was convinced my precise, fundamental style of play would be a good fit. Jerry and his assistants had done their homework. I noted that they knew exactly my strengths and weaknesses.

I took a recruiting trip that summer to check out sunny Salt Lake City. On first glance, it was lacking the cultural diversity of Los Angeles, which made me regret my previous year's decision all over again. But on the other hand, it was pristine, pretty, and there was plenty of undiscovered territory to explore. Most of all, I looked forward to the chance to prove myself all over again.

Besides, what kind of a greedy bastard could complain about the offer, which was just shy of the Lakers deal—$12 million over four years, guaranteed?

There must be some kind of unwritten rule among players. Whenever they sign a huge guaranteed contract, they insist their hoop dreams have nothing to do with money. All they care about is "love of the game." Or perhaps taking care of their families, leaving aside what we all know: With an average NBA contract, a guy could take care of hundreds of families and still have enough money left over to live like a king. That's why it's refreshing when someone comes right out and acknowledges the truth.

A lot of guys do play for love of the game. But it burns me when they claim that they play *only* for the game, that they love it so much they would play for free. They are inevitably quoted spouting such nonsense as they squabble over the extra $250,000—on top of the $19 million they have already been offered.

For me it was never the rags-to-riches story you hear so much about. It was far more about fulfilling a goal, about proving my critics wrong, about being the first Brit to have a real career in the NBA, about a shot at a title. More than anything, I wanted to prove that even the unlikeliest kind of person, coming from the most improbable circumstances, could make it to the top. It was an act of revenge for fat, tormented kids everywhere.

Certainly it was also about making Mum proud, even after she was gone. Extraordinary achievement is the ultimate homage a child can pay to a parent. And after all her devotion and sacrifice, she deserved nothing less.

I knew basketball itself would never satisfy me. Some find joy in the sound of a bouncing ball, the roar of the crowd, the intensity of competition, the advantages of stardom. I, however, found that the game just didn't hug me back.

CHAPTER 22 ●●●] The System

Leaving Orlando was one of the hardest things I'd ever done in my life. I packed my bags, sold the house—the closest thing I'd had to a family home I'd lived in since I left Manchester as a teenager.

I had a tearful farewell with Martin and Jeff, who were starting the college phase of their lives. We would remain close. After all, I still considered them my kids. But it would never be quite the same. I said goodbye to teammates, now scattered around the country.

It was all part of the heartless business I'd chosen. But that didn't make it any easier.

I spent much of the summer in Scottsdale with Warren, getting ready for the season. By the time September rolled around, I was actually looking forward to starting over with my new team and proving that the Magic had made a grave mistake by not fighting to bring me back.

With my old friend from Arizona, Nancy, I loaded up my rented Chevy Tahoe and set off on the 14-hour journey. It was thrilling to reach the crest of foothills and watch the world open up. We listened to Cirque du Soleil's *La Nouba* as the sun turned orange and sank under the horizon.

There were the usual spats with Pantz, as Nancy is known, because she is as technically challenged as I am overbearing. I would demand an instant image of some quickly disappearing vista while I sped along at 90 mph (as fast as that piece of junk would go on any kind of grade). She fumbled with the digital camera while I barked completely unhelpful instructions and then declared, "Damn it! *Damn it!* Oh, It's too late, you've missed it!"

The drive itself was uneventful until we passed the Utah border and were clocked at about 30 mph over the speed limit. An amiable state trooper let me go with a warning, after I gave him another autograph for his "wall of fame." That ballplayer's get-out-of-jail-free card sure did come in handy sometimes.

We arrived early that morning in Salt Lake City. After a few hours of sleep, I switched on the hotel television to see images of planes flying into the World Trade Center. Nancy groggily emerged from her bedroom, and we watched, transfixed, as the towers collapsed.

In the lobby, guests gathered to watch Fox's "fair and balanced" reporting. It was clear from listening to the commentator and to the people around us that from that day on it would be a very different experience to be an outsider inside the United States.

For the most part, I'd been welcomed in the States with open arms, even in the most conservative American communities. But now it was obvious the nation would become a little more suspicious, a little less generous, especially since the right-wing president would soon lead a domestic and international crackdown.

At any rate, it really did put what I saw as my misfortunes in perspective. We were all, every single one of us in the lobby that day, among the lucky ones.

●●●

After my first workout with the team a few days later, John Stockton sauntered across the gym and stuck out his hand. "I have a good feeling about you," he said with a smile. "You're gonna have a great career here."

Coming from Stockton, one of the game's finest point guards, that meant a lot. Even a natural cynic like me had to admit it was pretty cool to be on the same court with guys like Stockton and Malone, inside a storied franchise.

The whole city seemed excited about my arrival. The team needed someone to take the scoring burden off the big two, and with my ability to score facing the basket, the Jazz had brought in what fans hoped was the answer.

Even my quirks seemed to go over well. I wowed 'em in my first press conference, inspiring this over-the-top description in the *Salt Lake Tribune*:

> [Amaechi's] musical tastes range from Ella Fitzgerald
> to Eric Clapton; he designs gardens; he loves to cook,
> and eat foods that are unhealthy, such as cheesecake

and donuts; he is a cartoon addict, but also religious about watching the Discovery Channel; he doesn't much like jock talk, but he will jabber for hours about national drug policies, juvenile crime, and social problems; he says he "teeters between being opinionated and arrogant," yet he attempts to be open-minded; he listens to opera before games, and he writes poetry, including this little ditty: "The Earth is a stone, every crack a niche. To look is to know, to care to be rich."

Now, for most Americans such traits would not be considered a big deal. But for a basketball player, it was supposed to make me stand out.

And they didn't know that half of it.

●••

After years of dominance, the 2001 Jazz were on their last legs. The franchise cornerstones, Stockton and Malone, were nearing 40, the final buzzer even for the elite. Jerry Sloan hoped to make one more run at a title before dismantling and rebuilding the team, and I was to be a key piece of the puzzle, backing up both Malone and my old buddy Greg Ostertag. It was a bonus to be reunited with the massive teddy bear of a center.

If Stockton was the savvy part of the team—distributing the ball according to Sloan's game plan—Malone was its soul.

One afternoon during preseason, we headed to Malone's grand lodge on the outskirts of town for a Jazz tradition: a race across the rugged foothills of his huge property. Despite all his achievements, he still ran those hills like a mountain goat. I admired his relentless drive to be the best power forward the game had ever seen, even after he'd long ago achieved that status.

Lapping everyone, Karl made us all look like benchwarmers without making us *feel* that way. Great players have a tendency to apply their own standards to teammates who can't possibly achieve it, a tendency that ends up hurting the supporting guys. Karl had a rare ability to realize that even if everyone put in equal effort, the results would not match his own. So there was a healthy sense of accomplishment when, after the run, the guys hung out on his massive porch as we downed cold beverages, including more of the dreaded iced tea. We'd managed to survive on his training ground.

Even though I was to be his backup, I hadn't said a word to him beyond hello. Back in my college days, my dorm room was covered with Malone posters and I collected articles about his famous work ethic, hoping it would somehow rub off on me. In the earliest photos from my years in the States, I'm invariably wearing a Jazz T-shirt. So I was feeling slightly intimidated—an exceedingly rare sensation for me.

Karl towered over me. I was sitting by myself on his porch with a huge glass of ice water in my hand when he turned to me.

"You don't say much, do you, Amaechi?"

I wanted to impress him with something witty. "Uh, no," was all that came out of my mouth.

Malone chortled.

Usually I'm quite chatty. It was just that I'd yet to feel comfortable joining in, and it wasn't that easy to make the transition to a new team at a relatively advanced age. Every one of the six members of the team on the trek that day were veterans, so I was still in the "initiation" phase, not included in the macho banter or the inside jokes.

It's not that I'm too English to "shoot the shit." Rather, by that point in my career, I'd learned that it made sense to get the lay of the land before throwing in my two cents. Nobody liked a loudmouthed newcomer.

It didn't take long for Karl and me to bond over a surprising topic: politics. We never saw eye to eye, yet after every discussion I was left with the impression that it would be a mistake to underestimate this man—on or off the court. Like Ben and Bo in Orlando, he was the kind of guy you knew had your back, no matter what.

We were the personification of the red-blue divide. He was an NRA spokesman; I loathe guns. He was anti-abortion; I'm pro-choice.

"Raging liberal," he'd deride me with a big grin.

"Extremist," I'd shoot back.

Those differences I could accept. What bothered me was the rampaging xenophobia that he wore as proudly as his knee-length Armani black leather jacket. Like a lot of black athletes who become rich and famous at a young age, Malone identified more as an all-American patriot than an outsider. So much so that he saw criticizing the nation that had made his dream possible as treasonous.

As far as he was concerned, the world rotated around the United States; everything that mattered happened in *his* nation. Having played around the world, I tried to help him see how provincial such as attitude really was. This attitude sometimes made him indifferent to the suffering of others, even the way in which some minority groups are made to feel like outcasts in their own country.

The Twin Tower attacks intensified our differences. He was an ardent advocate of Bush's "bring 'em on"-style war on terror, a campaign I found reckless and counterproductive. I was uncomfortable with the American (and in its wake, British) tendency to demonize the enemy, and to seek to eliminate it with military might alone. It was as if the president could only see the world as some kind of international sports contest, played with missiles and bombs, in which there could be only one victor.

The West needed to be smarter and better, not simply stronger.

The Jazz, after all, were perennial contenders not because they were the most talented team, but because they were the smartest. Karl of all people should have known that.

●••

When it comes to social issues, Karl is best known as the superstar who denounced Magic Johnson's comeback bid after he tested HIV-positive. Though it had been well established that the virus can't be transmitted casually, Karl triggered a health concern when he refused to take the court with his old friend, as if Magic was some kind of a leper, not a courageous ballplayer who simply wanted a fair shot at playing the game to which he had contributed so much.

This is the old perception vs. reality problem. I'm HIV-negative, but for all he knew I could have been positive when I played against him. Karl would never have known the difference. Magic, because he was open about his status, became the target, the scapegoat.

Karl's backward stance came at a time in the early 1990s when Americans were crying out for leadership. He could have given jocks everywhere permission to declare: "Damn. If this truck-drivin', gun-totin' redneck can get with the program on HIV, then so can the rest of us."

No one would describe Karl as a follower, at least on the court, but in this case he refused to lead. Actually, he was leading us backward.

Ignorance is always bad. But ignorance combined with power and wealth is toxic. The NBA knows this, which explains the extensive training they provide. Today, an HIV-positive player would be less likely to face overt barriers. The sensitivity training offered young ballplayers is up-to-date on everything from STD prevention to how to handle the fame and riches about to be lavished on them. It may be that this program protects the NBA image (and bottom line), but it also shows an awareness of the impact these young men have on the outside world.

For the sake of team unity—not to mention self-preservation—I kept a lid on my disappointment with what Karl had done to Magic. It didn't make sense to hold a grudge long after Magic had forgiven him.

That year I was honestly more frustrated with Malone's pro-NRA politics. HIV discrimination was diminishing, slowly but surely; gun violence was skyrocketing. Those newspaper photos of the gun-toting Malone were not exactly the message he needed to be sending when bullets were killing kids by the thousands.

When it became clear that it had been a colossal mistake to turn down the Lakers, I consoled myself with the notion that I'd play for another great coach, Jerry Sloan. And there was little question that Sloan was a terrific strategist who found ways to win, no matter what.

I'd learned the hard way that great coaches do not necessarily make great human beings, though. And playing for Jerry was nothing like observing him from the opposing bench.

Up close, I was shocked. From our first meeting, I couldn't help confusing, in my mind, "Sloan" and "sallow," as in Coach Sallow. He was pale and withered, a body gradually losing the war it had waged against the world. Yet he had the arrogance of an aging gunslinger who'd survived so many bullets that no one dared challenge him.

Except, in my mind, he was one of the bad guys. Before I'd even had a chance to prove myself, he'd taken a rather massive dislike to me.

I suspect the antipathy to being challenged was one reason. Coming off my best seasons and having played across the globe, I wasn't going to accept any shit.

I played solidly, but it soon became clear he had no interest in working me into what was known simply as "the system." Basically, there was one way to play in Utah, one scheme that, I was told repeatedly, had "always worked."

Well, it worked for Malone because it was designed for Malone and that little matter that he was one of the greatest players ever.

I was no Karl Malone.

Sloan had signed me because I had some nifty low-post moves, a smooth jumper, and, despite not being able to jump over a small cat, I could score pretty consistently from 15 feet in. I lacked Karl's dominating presence (who doesn't?), but I was always capable and eager to contribute.

When I brought up the way in which the system didn't work for me, Jerry looked like he wanted to shoot holes right through my heart. With every passing day he was more pissed. If I had a good game, it would be followed by DNP-CD. (Did not play; coach's decision.)

During one home game, I got slapped with a three-second violation. "Stupid fuckin' cunt," he screamed at me.

Jerry loved the "c" word. Even Stockton and Malone were awarded that particular slur from time to time. So much for according respect to future Hall-of-Famers.

Putting aside the inherent misogyny of that epithet, Jerry's managerial skills were atrocious. The notion that he could motivate by name-calling showed how out of touch he really was. Perhaps that tactic work with scared school kids. But we were grown men.

Not to mention the fact that we all had guaranteed contracts, so he might as well have been spitting in the wind anyway.

"Fuck you, Jerry. Fuck you!" I screamed right back at him.

So it wasn't my articulate best. But I needed to show him that even a mild-mannered British guy could trash talk right back at him.

Jerry practically hit the Delta Center roof. Yanking me from the game, he pointed a long, bony finger in my face and ordered me out of the arena. I refused, planting myself in the middle of the bench. What was he going to do, have me arrested?

After the game, he suspended me.

It wasn't even the epithets that bothered me. He was telling me I couldn't get his respect no matter how hard—or how well—I played. That created a no-win situation for both of us. Worse still, for the team itself.

Jerry's inconsistency was notorious. He would scream at players—especially Ostertag and me—and then apologize. Apologize to Ostertag, that is, but never to me.

It seemed I was the one guy he refused to mollify after one of his screaming fits. So I made a point of sitting down in his trophy-dominated office for long, thoughtful discussions about what I need to do to get more playing time, to stay in his good graces and in his rotation. It was difficult to get a hearing; a large and distracting posse of yes-men always surrounded the great Sloan.

He'd listen, agree, and I'd get more floor time for a few games. Then, before I saw it coming, he'd relegate me to the end of the bench again.

Or he'd play me for 75 seconds of scrub time—when the outcome has already been decided—the ultimate show of disrespect for a veteran ballplayer.

I'm a thoroughly non-violent person by both temperament and philosophy, but I couldn't help fantasizing about a Latrell Sprewell moment.

●••

Looking back, I realize that more than anything, Sloan reminded me of my maternal grandfather. There was a physical resemblance, but it was the emotional one that bothered me most.

When we moved in with Grandad and Grandma Hall at their house in Stockport, I was all of 4. We turned their grandparents' peaceful existence upside down, making Grandad a little cranky and lot resentful. He berated, screamed, and cursed at us, even though we were just kids.

Grandma Hall, however, loved having us around. She and Mum were the only thing standing between his daily terror and us.

"Now, Harold, they are only children," she would scold during one of his periodic tirades. This gentle but uncompromising

"Harold" refrain would inevitably bring all activity in the house to a halt. A moment later, the cacophony resumed.

To be fair, we three kids ran amok. I was fast becoming a very big child, triggering a clumsy phase where everything I touched shattered. So I understand why Harold refused to call us by our given names, referring to us instead by the generic "monsters," contempt dripping from curled lip.

"DE-MOL-ISH!" he'd scream, but only when neither wife nor daughter was around. "That's all you do: DE-MOL-ISH!"

Granddad cast a shadow of fear over us. We weren't a bad lot, but he had a knack for making us feel like the worst kids in the world when Grandma wasn't around to keep him in check.

As a male role model, something my childhood lacked, he left a lot to be desired.

Perhaps his attitude helped me better understand the kids whom I would eventually mentor. Without the warmth from Mum and Grandma to temper Harold's coldness, I might have ended up as furious as he was.

Coupled with the bullying I experienced at school and a father who threatened to kidnap us, I understand the reason for my utter disdain for sadistic coaches. Discipline is important, but it can be meted out in a fair and respectful way. Motivation through fear, abuse, and intimidation is soul destroying, and has no place in any modern workplace.

●●●

One day after practice, Jerry confronted me in the hallway. "John, I need to ask you something straight out: Do you love the game of basketball?"

I'd rehearsed my answer to this question for some time, because I anticipated the case he was building against me. "I'm a pro," I replied. "It doesn't matter how I feel about the game. It has no effect on how I play."

I could tell by the look on Jerry's face that wasn't the right answer. I'd declined the opportunity to parrot back what he wanted to hear. Silly me, I figured he'd rather hear the truth. If he knew the right answer, why'd he bother to ask?

"If you don't love this game, you don't deserve to play," he said. Then he turned his back and walked away.

I'd left home at 17 to live alone in the American Midwest for a shot at the pros. I'd left my mother's deathbed to play in a game. I'd sacrificed my personal life. I'd gone without love and companionship. I'd spent years hearing people insist, "Fat English kids don't belong in the NBA." These were some of the many sacrifices I made to play in the NBA. Surely Jerry understood something of this. After all, he did his due diligence before handing out owner Larry Miller's millions.

Yet here he was accusing me of dogging it. If there was any justice in this world, Jerry would have burst into flames just for suggesting I didn't deserve to be there.

Jerry raged against players whom he thought didn't play hard enough, claiming they were undermining coaches across the league. If we lost two or three in a row, he would stride into practice yelling, "You fucking assholes are trying to get me fired. I'm not losing my job because you guys aren't hustling."

During one of these job-insecurity diatribes, Karl looked at me and smirked, "If only we were so lucky." Then he went back to the posture he'd long ago adopted: working diligently on his game while pretending Jerry didn't exist.

The whole "love the game" debate was absurd. Did one of the game's most distinguished coaches honestly believe that the guys who'd played for him over the years would love basketball if they were not raking in the big bucks?

I knew for a fact that plenty didn't enjoy the game, because they told me so. Several of my teammates joked that they deserved their fat bank accounts, fancy cars, and mansions just to "put up with Jerry's shit."

Why does the performance of so many players decline after they sign multiyear guaranteed deals? It's a little thing called human nature. Plenty of guys—Karl Malone and John Stockton are obvious examples—play hard no matter how much they make. Other guys lack the discipline. Predicting which player falls into which category is the key to scouting.

The NBA's passion play is a farce in which players are expected to fulfil the delusions of fans. The truth is, some guys play for love of the game. Some for love of the money. Some for love of the fame. Some for love of the women, a by-product of fame and money. All these motives fuel passion and dedication, but they are not necessarily what fans have in mind when they imagine taking the court themselves.

Fans want to see the passion they have reflected in the players. They demand soaring drives, off-balance three-pointers, behind-the-back passes, towering dunks, and dramatic celebrations. It's not enough to be a solid professional—the key to any winning team. Since the fans are, in some ways, paying our salaries, they believe we *owe* them. They believe they are paying us for doing something they would do for free.

The fan sitting at home watching the game on his big screen, beer in hand, wants us to love the game like he does. But that's egocentric. If he knew why we really play the game, for the most part, he might not love the game. He might not even watch it. Players don't perform for Little Johnny in the fourth row. Love isn't the X-factor between good and great.

The reason Derrick Coleman was no Karl Malone wasn't because Karl had a bigger passion for the game; it was because Karl ran the foothills all summer while Derrick partied with his posse. That's a matter of will, not love.

By and large, players give the fans—and the television cameras—what they demand. They give them a show. They learn to walk the walk. What they don't always give them is solid basketball. No wonder fundamental play has declined in recent years, and that even some of the best players can't play D if their lives depended on it.

In the privacy of the locker room, players talk openly about how hard it is to sustain dedication through the grueling, 82-game season. It's an absolute fallacy that we thrive on sweat, the preseason conditioning, the endless cross-country travel, the boredom and loneliness of empty hotel rooms, on the games in which your ankles feel like they are going to snap and your knees explode.

Kids who love the game are playing it on the street or in a park somewhere. And even for these young men, there is an aspirational element. They are playing for status, for camaraderie, to tone their bodies, to impress chicks (or, for that matter, other guys), for a shot at the big time. Once they get there, their motives become more complicated.

The problem was not my commitment to the game. I was working as hard, with what I had, as anyone on the team. The truth is that Sloan and the Jazz management hadn't done their research—otherwise known as scouting. They could tell you all my court tendencies, how I played the game, and why I should fit into the system. But they knew nothing of my *character*. People might not know everything about me—I'd kept some things locked in the closet—but they know a lot. I'd never exactly been shy about expressing unorthodox opinions, in print or elsewhere. There was no way they didn't know my perspective on guns, war, race, or the fantasy world of the NBA.

In its first profile of me, the *Orlando Sentinel* explained that I kept basketball in perspective, refusing to allow it to dominate my life. A web search or a five-minute perusal of my own web site, where the articles were indexed, would have revealed my outlook.

I respect the game of pro basketball. I just don't think it's all that important. Sports, in and of itself, isn't a noble profession with any intrinsic value. It is noble only to the extent that it teaches ethical ideals, teamwork, discipline, appreciation of diversity—something that only happens when participants demand that it do so.

We're entertainers—sometimes very good ones—and that's worth something. But let's not confuse it with teaching or parenting or international diplomacy. The discipline of a well-coached team game can teach, to be sure, but that's not what we were doing out there in the Delta Center.

I wasn't going to be embarrassed by Jerry Sloan because basketball had a proper role in my balanced life, and I didn't blindly worship a game he'd made pretty much the entirety of his existence.

I had a sneaking suspicion my basketball philosophy was not the bottom line anyway. There was something else that bothered

Jerry about me, and me about him—something neither of us could articulate at the time.

It was only some months later that I was able to piece the real story together.

CHAPTER 23 ●●●]

The Only Show in Town

There was something to be said for starting over. I missed my sisters Muriel and Uki, my kids back home, and my Orlando teammates, all at the same time. Given my current situation, Doc Rivers was looking better than ever.

But off court I gained an element of anonymity, which had its advantages at a time when I desperately needed room to explore and build the kind of vibrant social life I'd started to have back in Manchester. Thanks to Jerry Sloan, I was rarely on the court where cameras would beam my image into living rooms.

Still, I was one of 12 members of the only show in town. And despite the infrequency of my court appearances, I got my share of autograph hounds and basketball gawkers. So I stayed away from the public places where athletes tend to be identified.

Even so, a six-foot-ten black dude walking down the street in one of the whitest places on earth gets plenty of attention. A six-foot-ten black dude walking down the street with a posse of flamboyant gay guys draws even more attention. For the first time in my American career, that was a problem I wouldn't mind having.

The more miserable my life became on the court, the more I yearned for a decent one off it. If I had to be in the repressive Mormon capital of the Western world—sitting at the end of the bench for a coach who called me by his favorite epithet—I might as well enjoy myself. A fabulous existence, I decided, was the best revenge. And I do mean *fabulous.*

I splurged on a huge loft in an old chocolate factory—hardwood floors, raw brick walls, floor-to-ceiling windows. It literally took up half the block. It was, I realized the moment I laid eyes it, the perfect party pad, conveniently located next to Naked, one of the city's coolest nightclubs. The restaurant P.F. Chang's and the city's best art gallery were also right down the block.

My mood darkened when I realized I lacked the friends to fill the space. I hungered for a chance to interact without the NBA façade that causes you to be treated as an object—a celebrity commodity rather than a fallible, complicated human being. Most fans make little effort to get to know the real you, so they can preserve their illusions about professional athletes. More than anything, I needed friends with whom I could be myself and who would treat my secrets with the respect they deserved.

Now that I had a guaranteed contract, I felt liberated. In Orlando I'd avoided my kind of crowd because I worried about repercussions for my kids, my contract negotiations, my youth basketball center back home in Manchester—for my own tenuous sense of self. Now I was ready to venture out.

I still had plenty to lose. All the same fears—real and imagined—persisted, to a somewhat lesser degree. Utah employers are legally free to discriminate on the basis of sexual orientation, and there was plenty of evidence my employer, Jazz owner Larry Miller, under the guise of Mormonism, might do just that, having made his antipathy to gay people clear. (That never stopped his NBC affiliate, the source of much of his wealth, from airing the lucrative *Will & Grace*. Later, in 2005, one of Miller's movie theaters banned *Brokeback Mountain*. I always wondered why in his moral universe one was acceptable and the other was not.)

I hadn't felt this low since my exile in Athens. I truly believe that a soul can handle only so much heartache. After a while, your unconscious mind finds any means necessary to stop the pain. This is my explanation for the George Michael phenomenon—getting busted and outed in one fell swoop.

●••

I made a bee-line to the Avenues, the city's so-called "alternative" neighborhood. It was a place where Salt Lake outcasts—liberals, secularists, non- and lapsed Mormons, and gays—headed to find solace. The residents were united in their diversity.

The Avenues reminded me of the village in the film *Pleasantville* after it comes alive with color. Cottages with perfectly manicured lawns were festooned with rainbow flags. In winter, trees bent under the weight of snow; in the summer, flowers blossomed. The neighborhood was so picturesque, its inhabitants imagined it was compensation for living under Utah's harsh and judgmental moral code.

During my second year in Utah, wandering around Ninth Avenue the morning before a night game, I stumbled across the

Coffee Garden. It was not strictly a gay hangout, but if we go by the "black rule" (where, if a certain percentage of a neighborhood is black, it becomes a black neighborhood), then it could be considered gay space. It's also a place where nerdy University of Utah professors, aging hippies, and hip opposite-sex couples and their kids congregate.

Before long I was a regular. I'd set up my laptop and spend an entire afternoon lounging in the easy chairs, sipping Earl Grey, chatting with the staff, surfing the web.

Across the street was Cahoots, one of those off-color card places that are hardly Hallmark. It sold everything from erotic magazines to rainbow flags to Mormon Temple shot glasses— vaguely blasphemous in a town where temperance is actually considered a virtue.

One day, not long after I arrived in Utah, I was hanging out there with Nancy. Her gregariousness is a nice complement to my sense of reserve, and I've always loved the fact that she embraces the fag-hag label.

Nancy already seemed to know everyone in town, and she introduced me to the Cahoots manager, Ryan, who acted as my unofficial social ambassador to Salt Lake City. Ryan, his then-boyfriend, Steve, and I quickly became inseparable.

Ryan was tall, perma-tanned, and generally outrageous. He worked out with the ferocity of a pro athlete, resulting in a sculpted body with four percent body fat. Like most of the friends I made in Salt Lake, he was a lapsed Mormon. Some had been excommunicated. Others, like Ryan, ran screaming from the fold.

I never actually announced, "Yep, Ryan, I'm gay," in so many words. He told me later he wasn't sure, until he came round and heard the strains of Karen Carpenter coming through the chocolate factory front door and then, once inside, found the place filled with fresh-cut flowers.

The rainbow towel in the bathroom confirmed his suspicions. Ryan commented that I must have been the only jock in history to "towel off with multiple colors while singing along to 'We've Only Just Begun.'"

Through Ryan, I fell in with a great crowd. These guys were highly protective of my privacy and would carefully vet everyone I met. Since I was still reluctant to venture out too far, everyone came to *my* closet—literally. (At 2,500 square feet, it was one of the biggest in history). Yet I found it frustrating to say goodbye at 11 p.m. as they headed out the door to dance the night away. That, I told myself, would have to wait until the moment my contract expired.

I made it a rule to avoid public places where I might be identified, even though on some level it made no sense; anyone I saw in a gay club likely would be there for the same reason I was. Accustomed to a repressive atmosphere where people are ostracized merely for being gay (or even suspected to be gay), it was a community that placed a tremendous value on discretion. Everyone, it seemed, had something to lose. That fact didn't stop them from enjoying every hour of every day. In fact, they were the most outrageous bunch I'd ever come across.

While my "posse" partied, I'd sit home on my leather chair reading and watching BBC America on my flat screen, cursing the constraints of my profession and dreading another confrontation with Coach.

The whole group became so close that, back in Scottsdale during the off-season, a bunch of the guys would make the trip to visit me. That house turned out to be just the party pad I hoped it would become when I was designing it in Athens.

When I look back at the photo albums from those days, I'm amazed at the ubiquity of the parties. There are image after image of smiling, laughing revelers, a mix of my Utah and Arizona buddies. My career may have been on the downside—I was on the court about as often as the ball boys—but I was having the time of my life away from the game. Those grumpy social conservatives who continue to insist that gay life is lonely and unhappy have obviously never met my friends.

It was the first time I'd lived relatively freely among my gay peers, and I luxuriated in every second. No one cared how tall I was or whether I was in the starting lineup tomorrow. They knew how to look past sports, wealth, and status—not to mention my stats, which were *way* down that year. They didn't care about my minutes per game or how many boards I was pulling down. In fact, for all they knew MPG was some new party drug.

Yet they also were the kind of guys who'd been excluded from the inner circle of male athletics since they were kids, and though I could hardly claim to epitomize that clique, I could see the thrill of the experience in their eyes at the mere proximity—even if they didn't necessarily know Malone from Magic.

I often snagged them family room passes, and the guys would hang at halftime and after the game. Ryan spent so much time there that he grew close to the wives and girlfriends of my teammates.

I would spot him hugging them goodbye when we departed the stifling atmosphere of a Jazz postgame locker room. There were the occasional raised eyebrows, especially when Ryan screamed "nice ass!" as I drove the lane.

I even had an experience unfamiliar to my life in the States: sex. I had a memorable drunken night with an adorable wrestler (what is it with those guys?) from the University of Utah. He showed up at one of my parties and refused to leave.

Gay men, after all, are really just men, and it was more than a little frustrating for much of my career to switch on the TV in some strange town and listen to preachers denounce "evil, promiscuous gays" shagging out of control while simultaneously hearing, through hotel walls, married hetero teammates loudly and enthusiastically screwing women who were *not* their wives.

●••

It's hard to overestimate the stranglehold of the Latter Day Saints on the state of Utah. With the majority of the residents, the church had major say in everything from the composition of the legislature to what was considered appropriate attire. Which is why I was astonished that the city is the hippest, gayest place east of San Francisco. (Okay, so there's not a lot in between.)

Frankly, the Jazz fan base isn't all that different from that of Coffee Garden. You can't throw a basketball into a crowd without hitting a gay man or a lesbian. Dozens of season ticket holders who sat directly behind the bench were same-sex couples. I knew they were gay because they'd show up at some of my parties. (One of my guests even turned out to work for Senator Orrin Hatch.)

The gay Jazz fans I know are some of the wealthiest in town. Going to a game, ensconced in the front row, was their way of communicating to the city that *we are everywhere*, even where we are unwelcome. (It worked both ways: Larry Miller was only too happy to take their money.)

Yet the Mormon majority seems blithely unaware of this flamboyant minority in its midst. They see same-sex couples walking down the street hand-in-hand. They drive by parts of town where every other Victorian house is festooned with rainbow flags. They see joyfully gay men pouring in and out of bars and clubs.

And at the same time, they don't see it. They're oblivious.

I loved watching the LDS majority dancing to the Village People's "YMCA" during timeouts. Did they have no idea what the song is about? I would put my head down during that campy classic, lest I make eye contact with Ryan and double over in laughter at the ridiculousness of it all.

Since same-sexers don't fit into the notion of Mormon utopia, we don't exist. The closest analogy I can think of is how Manchester residents deal with the year-round rain. If someone from the outside suggests that it rains all the time in Manchester, we deny it.

It's easier to live in denial than to accept reality. In much of Utah, gays are nothing more than a bothersome rainstorm.

To me, they were salvation.

●●•

The church, however, seemed enlightened compared to some of my teammates. Homosexuality is an obsession among ballplayers, trailing only wealth and women. They just didn't like "fags"—or so they insisted over and over and over again. It soon became clear they didn't understand fags enough to truly loathe them. Most were convinced, even as they sat next to me on the bus or plane or threw me the ball in the post, that they had never met one.

Over time, I became convinced that anti-gay prejudice is more a convention of a particular brand of masculinity than a genuine prejudice. Homophobia is a ballplayer posture, akin to donning your "game face," wearing flashy jewelry, or driving the perfect black Escalade.

Toward the end of the season, the team bus pulled in to a West Coast city, when I noticed a huge billboard towering over the road: SOMEONE YOU KNOW IS GAY. The minute I spotted it, I pulled off my headphones. I knew there would be chatter and I wanted to hear what the boys would came up with this time. Sure enough, a cacophony of shock and horror poured forth.

"If my kid grew up gay, I'd throw him into the street."

"I don't know any fuckin' fags."

"That's disgusting—two guys together."

The comments deteriorated from there.

They sounded all the notes expected of a ballplayer. I had my back to the guys, so I decided to keep my thoughts to myself. I put my headphones back on. Nothing I could say was going to enlighten them.

On more than one occasion back in Orlando, I'd gone out of my way to confront teammates who spouted anti-gay slurs. As a leader on that team, both in the locker room and on the floor, I felt it was my duty to stand up and be counted whenever someone went off on a tangent that was detrimental to our cohesion.

This time, relegated to Jerry Sloan's doghouse, I lacked the credibility to speak up.

●●●

Friends often marvel at the fact that my personal and professional lives remained largely separate for so long. I took steps to stay out of the limelight. But I never went out of the way to cover my trail.

When I was in New York during road trips, I'd check out Splash, a big gay club in Chelsea. In L.A. I hung out at the Abbey in West Hollywood, a space so visible that the patio is outdoors. I mostly avoided clubs when in my hometowns of Orlando and Salt Lake, and I never did the Internet dating thing, but those were about the only limits I put on myself my last couple of years in the NBA. All it would have taken was a single anonymous cell phone call from inside Splash to Page Six and I would have been toast. I was hiding, but in plain sight.

The boys in the bar respected my privacy, and I respected them. I made a point of never pulling the celebrity big foot routine, I drank responsibly, and I was friendly and open with almost everyone I met. I didn't give anyone any reason to try to hurt me.

My only brush with outing came during my second year in Utah. Out of the blue, I received an e-mail from a former boyfriend threatening to reveal a short relationship we'd had back in Britain. He also claimed to have had sex with pop star Robbie Williams, and he was going to the British tabloids with both stories—a kind of "twofer" he thought would result in a big payday.

I had no doubt the sleazy tabloids would pay for such information, and for a few weeks I lost a lot of sleep worrying about the inevitable questions if the story were published. I could already imagine the press conference I'd long dreaded, having to talk about my private life in a concrete way even I had yet to fully appreciate.

I wanted nothing to do with the situation. So I turned it over to my then-publicist back in London, who managed to convince this ex that by bringing John Amaechi into the story, he would compromise the real story, which was his alleged affair with sexy superstar Robbie Williams.

Since I am no Robbie Williams, it was not as difficult to stay out of the papers as one might think. First of all, in the age of unfathomable wealth, bodyguards, and gated communities, players don't hang out together as much as they once did. On the road, guys are assigned their own luxury suites. They drive, or are driven, back and forth from the arena in their own black-windowed luxury cars, some with chauffeurs.

Players do their own thing. We all had a common interest in keeping our personal lives off the front page. Call it the basketball version of "don't ask, don't tell."

Those bound by genuine vows of marriage and monogamy and children, especially veterans like Malone and Stockton, keep a pretty low profile. The unattached younger guys are screwing every pretty woman they come across, and while they love to advertise their virility to one another, there's also an advantage to keeping the details of their conquests to themselves.

I also had another convenient excuse all those years: I'm English. It's an old phenomenon, dating back to the film stars of the '20s, when audiences would ask: *Is he gay or is he British?* Every time I did something eccentric, like bringing my fabulously flaming friends to Jazz games, people would quip, "Oh, he's just English. Leave him alone."

Even so, by the end of my second Utah season, I was practically daring reporters to take the bait and out me. But it never happened. My sexuality, I felt, had become an open secret, which was fine by me. I'd left enough open to interpretation that suspicions were gaining momentum.

Over the years, I'd become increasingly adept at deflecting questions from the press. I practiced gender-neutral pronouns. When a reporter asked about my romantic life, I'd say, "I'm not with anyone at the moment." Or, "The kind of person I'd like to be with in the future is…" It was a little like Oscar Wilde on trial. I had to rehearse the answers to questions I could only imagine.

Like Robbie Williams, I also enjoyed playing with people a bit. And I got bolder over the years.

On the court I was always known as a solid defender, but now my guard was collapsing. One night before a game, Greg Ostertag, with whom I'd become close, asked me point-blank in the tunnel, "Ya gay, dude?"

"Greg, you have nothing to worry about," I said.

It was clear Greg couldn't have cared less. Looking back, I wish I'd confided to the gentle big man. I would have loved to spend more time with him and his family. Sharing such a personal truth with someone is the best way to build friendship.

The same goes for Andrei Kirilenko, our talented Eastern European small forward. I called him Malinka, Russian for "little one," and our non-American (or "*un*-American," as I was sometimes accused) backgrounds created an obvious bond.

Some time after Christmas of my last Utah season, as the team was sliding out of contention, Malinka instant-messaged an invitation to his New Year's Eve party, explaining he was only inviting his "favorite" friends. Then he wrote something that brought tears to my eyes: "Please come, John. You are welcome to bring your partner, if you have one, someone special to you. Who it is makes no difference to me."

I was hosting my own party that night, so I had to decline his sweet invitation. But I was moved. I had Ryan deliver Malinka a $500 bottle of Jean Paul Gaultier-dressed champagne.

The whole exchange was a revelation. Malinka's generous overture made the season more bearable. It also showed that in my own paranoia and overwhelming desire for privacy, I'd failed to give some of my teammates the benefit of the doubt. After all, it was always the boorish idiots who gave the rest of us athletes a bad name.

The sense of welcome and belonging, so often denied gay people even by their own families, meant the world to me, especially in the middle of a dreadful season in a strange desert state that in the end provided some of the best days of my life.

●●•

Jerry Sloan, however, was no Malinka, and he was busy nailing me to the backboard. By my second year with the Jazz, our feud became public. I sat on the bench 30 of 82 games, averaging less than ten minutes. Once again, my stat sheet was filled with the dreaded DNP-CD.

In January 2003, I was suspended again for supposedly not finishing a postgame bike routine. I did, in fact, complete it, but Sloan and his assistants didn't like that I was always quick to exit the building the moment my duties were finished, sometimes jumping into my car 15 minutes or so after the end of a game.

I always made sure to behave professionally, but Sloan apparently believed that my not loitering after games or practices was another indication of my lack of desire for the game. I may not have loved basketball the way he did, but to get where I was and where I wanted to go had required as much dedication as any guy in the game.

The game after my suspension, I had one of my best performances, scoring six points in a row as we overcame a 12-point deficit to defeat the Timberwolves in Minnesota. Obviously I was still motivated, and after the game Sloan admitted to reporters, "John played better and deserved a chance to play, quite frankly."

But as soon as he'd uttered those words, I was back on the bench yet again.

Not long after that, I gave an interview to *The Independent,* a London newspaper. The reporter asked why I wasn't playing more, and I responded with something one of Sloan's assistants had said to me, something I believed was the sentiment of the entire coaching staff. "You hate white people, you hate Americans, and you think you're smarter than everyone else," the assistant had told me at one point when we were talking about my attitude.

The quote did not go over well back in Utah. Sloan denied that anyone had uttered it, until one of his assistants actually copped to saying it. I'd known all along that it was true because he'd said it to my face.

Of course, I didn't hate white people at all. My mother was white; my first partner, Darren, was white. And I never thought I was the smartest guy on the court—it was just that smart, independent people threatened Sloan.

"I [like] basketball," I told *The Independent.* "It's an excellent job, but I question people who say they love their job as much as they love their family. And of course nobody does—they just say they do. The truth is that I'm far more professional than most basketball players. I don't go out and get hammered the night before a game, I don't philander on the road, but also I don't go in and say, 'I love this game so much I would play it for nothing.'"

The *Salt Lake Tribune* headlined its subsequent article, "Amaechi Speaks Ill of Sloan," as if I had dared to take on God himself.

The exchange gave Larry Miller a chance to pile it on as well. He was quoted saying that my mood was "dour" and that he would either trade me or reach a contract settlement, giving me my unconditional release.

It was a telling comment. What athlete wouldn't be "dour" about never getting to play the game he's spent the last decade perfecting? Was I supposed to be jumping up and down with glee? He was blaming me for a situation not of my own making.

Miller never bothered to get to know me. He was clearly backing up his high-profile coach, which, of course, is his prerogative. But it was unfair to label me a troublemaker, especially publicly.

In a way, those two were a good match. Miller was as much of a screamer as Sloan. After a tough loss, he would stride into the locker room and yell, "You fucking assholes. I'm gonna sue every fucking one of you for breaking your contract."

We would just roll our eyes and hurry out.

●●●

The day I was packing to depart at the end of the season, the chocolate factory manager confided in Ryan. "I wish that John had had a better time here," he said. "Perhaps if Sloan hadn't known about John's lifestyle."

There it was: I'd been sent packing because Sloan couldn't comprehend me, especially my sexuality. He dealt me unceremoniously to the Houston Rockets in exchange for Glenn Rice, a once-terrific scorer who was near the end of his career. I had been right. Even players with guaranteed contracts were vulnerable.

Unbeknownst to me at the time, Sloan had used some anti-gay innuendo to describe me. It was confirmed via e-mails from friends who worked in high-level front-office jobs with the Jazz.

Suddenly it all made sense. I'm not sure the great Sloan hated all "fags," though I'm pretty confident he's not exactly a gay advocate. He certainly hated me. No wonder I'd spent the bulk of the season with my ass planted firmly on the bench.

In the end, I asked myself why I'd bothered to hide at all. I'm not sure why I felt the need to stay away from those darkly alluring American nightclubs, where my friends celebrated their youth and their gayness. I suppose I feared the clubs' aggressive sexuality, their love of the glitter of celebrity and gossip.

Perhaps I feared I would enjoy them a little too much, see what I'd been missing out on all these basketball years, and never want to leave.

CHAPTER 24 ●●●⌉ The End Is Near

The view from the 26th floor of the skyscraper was a sight to behold. It was near the top of one of Houston's tallest buildings, and standing in front of the massive picture windows it seemed I could take in the entire vastness that is Texas.

I'd leased the place shortly after the Jazz shipped me to the Rockets, partly because the view was so enormous that it provided perspective on the world every time you even glanced at it.

Looking at the mass of humanity stretching for miles in every direction, I could see that my troubles were anything but unique, my joys fairly commonplace, even if this grand space I was now living in was not.

As my career was winding down in the fall of 2003, such perspective proved critical. I still marveled that a man like me would end up in a place like this—an awkward gay British kid raised by a single mother, playing for an amazing franchise in yet another stop on my tour of America's broiling, right-wing cities.

And as with my Salt Lake stint, I refused to succumb to the stereotypes of a dull, conservative town. I was determined to completely enjoy what I suspected might be my last stop in the NBA.

By that point, I'd made friends in Houston from previous road trips, and Ryan and my Salt Lake buddies promised to show up at my door with some regularity.

My new teammates were fantastic. I made a fast friend in Eddie Griffin. Though he was injured most of the time I was in Houston, he had enormous potential, and I hung out with him, admiring his ability to gain perspective even when he was languishing on the injured list.

I truly admired Jeff Van Gundy, a fiery head coach who nonetheless treated his players with enormous respect. I'd never met a man who took the play of his team more personally, and expected the absolute best in effort, yet never for a second doubted your good intentions. The notion that he would ever call anyone the c-word was laughable.

Basketball-wise though, that particular team wasn't a very good fit. It had five entrenched big men, led by the great Yao Ming, who at seven-foot-six was nearly a foot taller than me. Unless the entire front court was hit by lightning, it was clear I wouldn't get to see a lot of playing time.

My trade was a straight-up salary dump. Houston had unloaded an even bigger contract on the Jazz so that Sloan and Miller could be rid of the baggage they considered to be John Amaechi.

To his credit, Jeff made it clear I would play sparingly. And even though I had three years left on my contract at a hefty salary, I knew that spending another season on the bench would likely mean the end of my career. A 33-year-old veteran like me, coming off two subpar seasons, requires plenty of playing time to stay sharp, and the longer I sat, the less likely it was that another team would give me that rare shot at an opportunity.

I was determined to simply enjoy whatever time I had left, contributing however I could. At the same time, I prepared myself emotionally for the end. More important, now that I wasn't being verbally abused by a famous coach and derided as an anti-American traitor, my attitude was seriously transformed.

It was the first time I wasn't a regular part of the rotation (even Sloan threw me out there sporadically) since my rookie year, and by that point I'd had plenty of opportunity to observe how veterans handled such a demotion with grace and class. Or not.

Though I wasn't playing much, I worked hard in practice and in the training room. I strove to keep up the spirits of everyone around me—a critical and often overlooked responsibility of bench players, who often spend far too much time playing the victim rather than acting the loyal teammate.

Basically, I was a highly-paid cheerleader.

About halfway through the season I went on the injured list with a more or less fictitious shoulder injury. The Rockets wanted to play some younger guys, so they created roster space by placing me on the list.

The good thing was that it allowed me to stay behind in Houston while the team was on the road. I continued to work out at the arena. But the free evenings did wonders for my social life.

With the end of my public sports life in sight, I was even less secretive than I had been in Salt Lake. I could be spotted regularly at gay bars, even though I had an intense feeling of exposure when waiting in line outside, as if I would somehow be revealed right then and there. When guys I met in these venues realized who I was, the general attitude was, "Oh, that's nice."

Texas had a fairly pronounced history of gay-bashing and a huge hostility to "queers" (as we were known in parts of the state), but it also boasted pockets of great tolerance and diversity, a spirit that brought people together.

I was reminded of this contradiction when I first arrived. The Rockets assigned consultants to new players to assist in the acclimation process and to help them locate suitable housing. I was assigned a mother-daughter team. They were lovely people, but they went out of their way to identify themselves as Southern Baptists, which, perhaps unfairly, got me worried. To me, and to most people, I believe, religion is not something you necessarily share on your first meeting.

They objected when I told them I wanted to live in or near Montrose, a well-known gay neighborhood. It's no secret gay people long have carved out the best neighborhoods of any city. The proof of this is that they are generally the safest, most culturally vibrant, and community-oriented places in any metropolitan area.

Need urban regeneration? Call the gay team.

Montrose was no exception. Tree-lined streets were dotted with beautifully restored craftsman homes, all leading to a rollicking commercial district overflowing with people of all colors.

Yet my consultants warned me away. They were not interested in an objective analysis of living conditions. "That's just *not* a good area," they repeated, despite overwhelming evidence to the contrary. Essentially, they were trying to tell me that it was a gay neighborhood without actually having to directly express their hostility.

I rented the place I wanted anyway. I could feel their disappointment, but they kindly took me out to lunch, over which they talked incessantly about the Bible. To be sure, the good book is an interesting piece of literature; I've been known to dip into it myself from time to time. But they acted as though it was the only book ever written. So I slyly asked whether they had read anything else.

"Why would we?" they asked, practically in unison.

I realized it was a rhetorical question, but I answered it anyway. "Well, for perspective of course," I said. "How can you have an opinion if you know only one side? You have to look out more than one window to know where you stand."

They stared at me like I was crazy.

●••

Shortly before Christmas, Muriel and Ryan came for a visit. During the drive to pick them up at the airport, my cell phone rang. It was Van Gundy.

"John, I'm sorry to tell you this. You've been traded to New York."

Jeff thanked me for being "professional" about the whole situation and wished me well, saying that he'd seen far too many guys in that situation behave like "assholes," throwing off the equilibrium of the entire team. I was touched that he'd made the call himself. (He later sent a kind letter extolling me for being a "gentleman" in a difficult season.)

I talked over the news with Ryan and Muriel on the way back home. Basketball was a business, and I'd spent the last three seasons preparing emotionally for this eventuality. But it was still a lot to absorb, and I was grateful for the company of my sister and close friend.

I had no desire to start over again, especially in an even bigger media market, where I'd no doubt find myself alone in a crowd all over again. And I sure as hell didn't want to play for another team that didn't really want me. The Knicks had already made it clear my acquisition was essentially another salary dump.

The question of an athlete's retirement often devolves into public spectacle. A few retire too soon, with productive years left. But the majority wait too long, and fans end up remembering the bad years. Some are forced into retirement by management; others are begged to stay on.

I can't say that anyone other than Bill and my friends and family truly cared about my decision, one way or another. So I was on my own. There is no simple formula, no standard to go by. I was winging it, but as I searched my soul, lying in my dark loft that night, I *knew* I was done.

It is hard to explain exactly why I felt that way. It was sort of like drinking. I know at exactly which drink I've had enough, which drink will put me into hangover territory. I was afraid if I stayed one more season in the NBA, I might pass out and never wake up. It's probably a harder decision for those guys who have loved the game since childhood or who know little else.

Every year had been more and more of a struggle. This was not my life. I was never a basketball player; I just happened to be really good at it for awhile. I mostly looked forward to going home to hang with my friends, to take care of my kids, to work with future generations of children. And I wanted to do all this with at least a little more freedom to be myself when I chose. Basketball as an industry had simply not evolved to that point, and I alone was not going to force such a massive change. Even the millions of dollars I was bringing in couldn't make me enjoy the game. It just didn't add up any more.

I never suited up for the Knicks. A few months after the trade, Bill negotiated a buyout. He had received feelers from other NBA teams. There are always roster spots open for guys who know the league, who know how the game works, who know how to fill a role. And I was still young enough to qualify for one of those slots.

European teams were sniffing around, including a big offer from China—$1.5 million for only half a season. I still had some market value. But I'd already done a good job investing my earnings and I had a decent buyout, so money was not chief among my concerns. I was set, perhaps not for life, but at least for the time being.

Even if I'd saved nothing, I would have happily embraced a workaday existence. I'd never played for money or fame. I played to prove to people that I could accomplish something, that I could be special, to demonstrate I was not the loser I was sometimes made out to be.

Mission accomplished.

Perhaps I would only be in the basketball Hall of Fame for what was essentially a coincidence. But for a shining season in Orlando, I had been a fantastic NBA player.

It was more than enough to make a mother proud.

A few days after Jeff's call, I went out for a farewell New Year's Eve celebration with a group of friends. I finally crossed the threshold of one of those glittering nightclubs located in Montrose.

It was a massive smoke-filled space where no one did a doubletake upon spotting a big man—a soon-to-be-former-NBA big man. Muriel and Ryan were once again at my side, and a whole group of us took over the heart of the dance floor. Twisting above the bodies, basketball could not have seemed more remote from my life.

At the end of the night, standing on the balcony overlooking the floor, I surveyed the dancers yearning for connection, experiencing the exuberant kind of joy that too often eludes our everyday lives.

It was a sight to behold and, as far as I was concerned, better than a breakaway dunk before the home crowd.

EPILOGUE ●●•⌉ Role Models

At my basketball camp in Manchester last July, a big kid named Jeff was clearly struggling, but not on the court. He'd come to play, but he was dragged down by an unhappy home life that he could not leave behind.

Not long into the week, he burst into tears. I took him outside to try to console him, when he blurted, "You don't understand. This is my only escape. And it will be over soon."

I'd mentored enough young people by this point that, at the age of 36, three years removed from my last NBA season, I knew what to do. I was confident that, along with my staff and the 200 kids in camp, I could steer him through a difficult situation.

The most heartening reaction was that of his peers. Here was a six-foot-seven, 17-year-old boy, and no one was mocking him. No one was comparing him to large mammals or making fun of the fact that the young man was wearing his emotions on his sleeve.

In fact, they embraced him. I noticed other teens consoling him, putting their arms around his shoulder. They brought him a towel when he sweated, water when he was dehydrated. There was no taunting, no embarrassment. It was one of the sweetest things I'd ever witnessed—at my camp or anywhere else.

Sure, it would be nice to one day see one of these kids play in the NBA, or at least help reinvent moribund English basketball. But that's not what gets me up in the morning. It's a chance to change the culture, at least for a few kids.

The camp welcomes a broad cross-section of kids. Some are in healthy families and it just adds to their already happy lives. For others, like Jeff, it's an oasis.

It's fantastic to play a role in creating such an environment. Along with my excellent, hand-picked staff, we're giving kids hope for the future, the chance to see that life can be better if they work hard and play together as a team.

There is nothing intrinsically noble about sports. Three years after retirement, I still have nightmares that I will die young while still playing pro ball. In those dreams my tombstone reads, John Amaechi RIP: *He Put the Ball in the Hole Good.*

Though basketball dominated nearly two decades of my life, I still can't say my decision as a teenager to choose this career was the right one. From Joe and Ed and many others, I learned valuable lessons of tenacity and teamwork, which I impart to my young mentees (and even business clients) today.

But I also gave up a more normal life.

It says something that today, a leather basketball sits flat and unused in a corner of my house. I play now and then, of course. In the summer of 2006, I suited up for the UK team in the Commonwealth Games. I led the team, played well, and we won the bronze medal. But I can honestly say that will probably be the last time I wear a basketball uniform.

Basketball did provide at least one advantage, however, something far removed from the game itself. It has given me a platform to make a difference in the lives of young people, particularly through my charities.

I always knew that in the unlikely event that I achieved my goal, it only would be the beginning, not the end. If I did not achieve my goal, The Plan would form the basis of other pursuits.

I would like to consider myself a role model for these kids, even if many athletes shy away from the label for good reason.

Being a role model is a particularly loaded term for an openly gay man. Sadly, many parents do not want little Johnny to grow up to be a gay man like John Amaechi, no matter how exemplary he may strive to be in every other way.

How many times do hear about young NBA players who, having earned millions and achieved stardom, have nothing left to give? Why are so few players prominent, let alone eminent, after they retire?

That's why Charles Barkley actually is a role model, despite famously denying as much in the 1993 Nike ad. What he actually said is, "I am not a role model; parents are role models." Which is exactly where the emphasis should be. Yet for a man of Barkley's stature there's no getting around the label. Everything he does—from commenting on race and inequality in America to working with disadvantaged kids—screams role model.

My first season in the NBA, I ran into the Round Mound himself in the lobby of the Phoenix Ritz-Carlton. I was a raw rookie in awe of one of the game's greats. He wasn't the biggest, strongest, or fastest guy. He wasn't a great shooter until he had to be. He wasn't a great defender until his team required it. He willed himself to be one of three players to achieve the trifecta of 20,000 points, 10,000 rebounds, and 4,000 assists.

When I squared off against him on the floor, I had to remind myself to avoid idol worship. It was just business, I told myself, even though in my heart I knew it was so much more.

So when he walked over and slapped me on the back in the hotel lobby I was tongue-tied. "You guys are doing great," he said.

I was puzzled. At that point early in the season the Cavaliers were hardly great. Then I realized he meant Penn State. I was shocked that he actually knew where I'd gone to college. I was so flattered that before long my friends were quickly bored of hearing about how the great Charles Barkley actually knew where I played college ball.

It was a routine encounter for him. But for me it meant acceptance in a world he'd mastered. It was a great example of how a little kindness can win friends and influence people. I admire him, and not just for his rebounding skills.

There's really no way to avoid being a role model. If you have played in the NBA, even for a single game, you are a role model to somebody, somewhere. If you earned a ten-day contract and never played again, there are a dozen people in your hometown who suddenly view you in that light.

The question is not whether you are a role model. The question is whether you choose to be a good, bad, or indifferent one.

The bigger a star becomes, the more important it is to speak out. Take Michael Jordan. He's become not just a superstar but a publicly traded company, a massive brand in his own right, and everything he says and does publicly affects the people who hold shares in Michael Jordan. When scandal hits anywhere near him, Nike stock tumbles.

With fame and wealth comes responsibility. That's why I was disappointed Michael didn't confront Jesse Helms, the senator from his home state, North Carolina, during his bigoted re-election campaigns.

No one really cares what I think about the former senator—or about President Bush for that matter. A liberal Brit denounces the war in Iraq? Big fucking deal. But when a big star does it (thank you, Steve Nash), it actually means something.

In general, I'm disappointed that American and British athletes don't have more to say about the society in which they live, especially because so many came from backgrounds of relative deprivation.

There's a genuine concern about distracting athletes from a very difficult job. Agents and handlers routinely warn them that public opinions jeopardize corporate sponsorships and even their contracts. And it is definitely true that once you set yourself up publicly as a role model, people starting looking for ways to puncture your façade.

Others have simply forgotten from where they came.

●●●

Since I retired three years ago, I've been living mostly in London and occasionally in Scottsdale.

From my loft in Clapham—with a spectacular view of London—I can look down at the street at the boys pouring in and out of my local gay watering hole. In the few evenings I find time away from my projects, I sometimes even join them for a drink. Needless to say, I no longer look over my shoulder as I enter the place.

And though I am still intensely private, a few years back I actually celebrated the Manchester gay pride parade with some friends.

Sitting on the wall of the Manchester Cathedral (Pope Benedict XVI wouldn't have approved), I watched, cheering and smiling, as the often flamboyant marchers and floats passed. Then Sir Ian McKellen, one of Britian's greatest actors, appeared waving from the back of a pink convertible Cadillac. I felt a surge of pride that the great Gandalf would lay it all on the line for his beloved community.

It sounds corny, I know, but if a cynic like me can be inspired by the very act of *being out*, then perhaps I owe it to others to do the same.

After all, there is still much work to be done.